To Grandma
1886-1971

*whose life is a testament to loyalty, courage,
strength and determination.*

I honour the spirit within you.

Chasing Grandma

Barbara Young

Shoreline

Chasing Grandma
Copyright 2001: Barbara Young

Published by Shoreline, 23 Ste-Anne, Ste-Anne-de-Bellevue,
Québec, Canada H9X 1L1
Telephone: (514) 457-5733, Email: bookline@total.net
www.total.net/~bookline

Printed in Canada by AGMV Marquis, Québec
Designed by Maria Simpson

Photographs from collection of the author

Cover photo: Quarrier Home Children at Brockville, June 1896,
courtesy of Grace Bruce

Dépôt légal: Bibliothéque nationale du Québec, and the National
Library of Canada

National Library of Canada Cataloguing in Publication Data

Young, Barbara, 1931-
Chasing Grandma

ISBN 1-896754-15-5

1. Scott, Kathleen   2. Home Children (Canadian
Immigrants)—Biography.   3. Scottish Canadians—Biography.
I. Title.

FC2949.P63Z49 2001   362.7'086'91   C2001-900106-1
F1054.5.P59Y68 2001

"*Death is nothing at all. It does not count. I have only slipped away into the next room. Nothing has happened. Everything remains exactly as it was. I am I, and you are you, and the old life we lived so fondly together is untouched, unchanged. Whatever we were to each other, that we are still. Call me by the old familiar name. Speak of me in the easy way which you always used. Put no difference into your tone. Wear no forced air of solemnity or sorrow. Laugh as we always laughed at the little jokes that we enjoyed together. Play, smile, think of me, pray for me. Let my name be ever the household word that it always was. Let it be spoken without an effort, without the ghost of a shadow upon it. Life means all that it ever meant. It is the same as it ever was. There is absolute and unbroken continuity. What is this death but a negligible accident? Why should I be out of mind because I am out of sight. I am but waiting for you, for an interval, somewhere very near, just around the corner. All is well.*"

—*Author unknown.*
Quoted in September,
by Rosamunde Pilcher

The Home Children at Brockville, 1896

Contents

Prologue

*I*t started so innocently. At first, all I wanted were her parents' names for the family tree. Simple. Get the birth certificate, add her information to my chart. Done.

Not this time! She led me on a merry chase for eight years, without an answer to my seemingly uncomplicated question. Hours of work on my project turned into days, then months, and finally, years, as I followed the elusive trail of documents. Each new piece of information only led me deeper into the mystery surrounding Grandma's past.

I remember seeing her for the first time when I was about ten years old. She was staying at our house, as mother was sick, and our maid had left for factory work at higher wages. Short in height, she inclined to plumpness. Her hair was parted in the centre, plastered against her head, and wound into a bun at the nape of her neck; it was handsome, but severe. Her clothes were dark, yet well cut and neat; the only light coloured relief was her big white apron. Her voice was not soft, and when angered, harsh. She never, ever hit me, though; words were her weapons of chastisement.

Later, she was hired as housekeeper for an elderly gentleman, and moved to a house further up our street. When the grandchildren visited, we made the customary trip to the living room for presentation and approval of "he who sat in the best chair." It didn't take long, he wasn't interested in us, but grandmother insisted on our demonstration of good manners.

During the Second World War Grandma's hair turned grey, then white. She started wearing more colourful, becoming clothes. Always sparkling clean, her pink and white face shone with freshness and she smelled deliciously of cologne. Her kitchen smelled delicious, too. Milk, cookies, and bread with homemade jam were offered to the continuously hungry children. While the dinner roasted in the oven, or a pot simmered on the stove, we would chat about our activities.

If we had been good, we were allowed entry to her bedroom, where we were treated to the latest edition of *Good Housekeeping* or *Cosmopolitan* magazines. It was great fun to sit in a large chair by oneself, with a few moments to read a magazine. Grandma would pick up her knitting, and we didn't talk much, but kept each other company.

When she moved to the next town, three miles away, it was a long walk to visit her. This meant an earlier start, and lunch as reward. In time, mother insisted that it was my duty to visit once a week. Every so often a bicycle would be available and I could ride instead of hiking the distance. The routine was always the same: greet the old gentleman, then retire to the kitchen where it was cozy and warm. The food was always delicious. Grandma made wonderful meat patties with pan gravy, whipped potatoes and fresh cooked peas or other vegetables, with preserved fruit and cookies for dessert. I would waddle upstairs afterwards, replete, for a change, heading for her bedroom where again I could read, and she would knit. Occasionally, she would show me her treasures—a lovely brooch, a medal, a Scottish pin.

Grandma's employer died about 1956. After a few years on her own, she was moved to a small apartment. When her health deteriorated, she tried living with her daughter. It didn't work out, so she was lodged with various foster families in the Eastern Townships. Finally, ill, she was placed in a nursing home. Several years later, in 1971, she died.

The grandmother I remember was a hard-working, capable woman and extremely clean in personal hygiene as well as her household. Quietly dressed with care and taste, her clothing was of excellent quality. Careful with money, she waited until she could afford an item, then made it last. She was a good cook, who always used the best fresh ingredients. Most of all, she was very kind, although not demonstrative, to those she loved. I must have been one of them, as I was the recipient of exquisite gifts from her, throughout her life. At age 65 I still have the blue Waterman's pen and pencil set she gave me for high school. And I remember clearly the beautiful pale blue wool jacket we purchased together—a birthday present for an astonished, delighted teenager.

All the memories were useful in forming a picture of a known grandmother, but I wanted specific details to complete the family tree. There were, however, no documents in the family archives to substantiate events in her past, only memories of the stories she told us as children.

She told my sister and me she was born in Isle of Skye, Scotland; she told my brother Glasgow. She said her parents were killed in a fire and she was sent to live with relatives. Mistreated, she was removed from the home and placed in foster care by an Ontario child protection agency at age 12. At 16 she was turned out to earn her living.

Grandma told me she had worked in a munitions factory during the First World War. Her medal of service, issued to Women workers, has two bars, each bar signifying six months employment. The gold wedding band she wore, and which I now wear, was made by the same Toronto firm that manufactured the medal. After the war she worked as housekeeper for a Toronto doctor, then as a floor clerk for the Royal York Hotel.

She often talked about being descended from a long line of Stuarts, dating back to Bonnie Prince Charlie. She also complained of "people who took my money." We were usually amused at Grandma's romancing, sometimes impatient with her fantasy. Never did we question her more closely on what she may have meant. Her Aunt Sarah had been kind, she said, but she disliked her Uncle. Her tone was bitter whenever she told her story, and I believed her absolutely. There was no reason not to believe her. Our family had very strict rules about honesty, therefore the story had to be true.

That's all I knew. I don't remember any mention of Grandma's schooling, or anything she did for fun as a child; there were no photo albums or family pictures; three small photos of her young daughter were her wall decorations. There was no old furniture that might have belonged to her parents, no mementos, nor were there letters for grandchildren to read and enjoy. The past was a void. As I think about it now, her rooms were like those of a boarder, a transient who had few possessions, with no memorabilia of a family, such as could be found around our house.

Was Scotland truly her place of birth? Where did she spend her early childhood? Could I verify the names of her parents? Or where her parents had died?

I started looking for answers using the facts from the stories Grandma had told us. Nothing was found. Undismayed, I attributed it to my undeveloped research skills. One day, while figuring out my next line of enquiry, I received a letter from my brother. Among the enclosures was a handwritten page of notes he had unexpectedly discovered in the family Bible. We don't know when they were written, nor when Grandma gave Dad the information, but it had to be prior to her death in 1971.

There were no other family documents on Grandma, except for this one piece of paper which Dad had hidden in the Bible. I say hidden, because his family history work was in files, carefully labelled, for future reference by his children. We were mystified by his action because it seemed so unusual.

Nevertheless, using the notes, I set to work once more. Every entry was investigated in my attempt to validate Dad's information. The process took several years, as I learned how to seek out sources and follow the trail clue by clue. Sometimes the work was laborious, and yet, most of the time, I found it exhilarating. Finding a small lead was a triumph, encouraging me to look further, and I became very engrossed in the work.

The brief notes began with her name, Kathleen Scott née Wales, born July 1889 in Scotland. Her father was identified as Robert Wales, and her mother as Agnes, a Chicago-trained nurse. It was immediately apparent that there was a certain lack of clarity, since her mother's maiden surname had been added to the original entry, using block letters rather than script, with a caret to indicate the insertion. A similar problem arose later with the name of Grandma's husband. Very confusing!

After studying the data carefully, I decided to ignore the discrepancies and go ahead with the names and dates specified, and perhaps the reasons for the changes would become clear to me later on. During the subsequent investigations I could find no record in the Scottish or Canadian registers of Grandma being born, adopted, or baptized. Nor could I find a marriage or birth record for either parent, in Canada, Scotland or the United States.

Dad had tried to gather information, but his notes were contradictory, difficult to confirm, and as we later discovered, contained very flexible dating. We had no idea whether or not this was by design, or forgetfulness, on the part of Grandma or my father. This inability to easily confirm Grandma's parentage, however, merely strengthened my resolve. I was now determined to find her. But how?

Casting a wider net in my search for Grandma only brought further puzzles and contradictions. Dad's notes indicated Grandma had gone to live with her uncle, William H. Adams, in Ottawa in 1891, when she was six years old. I remembered Grandma affectionately mentioning her Aunt Sarah, and wondered if she was referring to William's wife Sarah. My investigation yielded a fount of detail on Adams family connections, but no clear information linking Grandma with them.

I was equally unsuccessful trying to document Grandma's marriage and the birth of her child in Toronto. Again, a lot was learned about other families, but no close connection with Grandma was established. And we still had not confirmed the names of her parents.

I was curious about her daughter's childhood as well. Mother never mentioned anything about those early years. Any stories she told us concerned her high school experiences. The few pictures I inherited from Grandma show her young daughter exquisitely dressed, well cared for and healthy. The clothes were all handmade, and beautifully tailored. Gran couldn't sew, and I wonder who made the lovely dresses. Was Gran able to afford them on a housekeeper's salary? And if not, who was?

It seemed sensible at this point to pause, review all the facts and summarize our progress.

When I finished writing a summary, I asked a friend to read my work and see if there was a pattern emerging that I did not see. The response was immediate. It was suggested Grandma might have been an orphan, perhaps one of the "Home Children." The lack of documentation and family relics, and the inconsistencies in the stories led to this conclusion. My next path became clear—find out all I could about Home Children, and see if my Grandma could have been one of them.

My study of the subject helped me to understand that Home Children were orphans, or children from families who could no longer care for them. Arrangements were made with various organizations and the Canadian government to bring the children to Canada. Boys were sent to farming families to work the land, girls to help in the household. An orphan's home, Bridge of Weir, had been founded near Glasgow, Scotland by William Quarrier during the 1870's, and some years later a receiving home, Fairknowe, was established at Brockville. I decided to investigate the possibility of Kathleen being a Quarriers child.

With this in mind I contacted David Lorente of Heritage Renfrew. David heads a non-profit, volunteer organization which assists those trying to find information on the backgrounds of the Home Children. I told him what I could about Grandma's background, and asked him whether it was possible Kathleen could have been a Home Child. David told me that her story perfectly fitted the profile. Then, with his help, I prepared and sent a letter of enquiry to Quarriers in Scotland. Once the letter was mailed, all we could do was wait and hope.

If we were able to confirm Grandma was one of the Home Children, the lack of documents, mementos and photographs would be explained. Her reluctance to discuss the past, as well as the differing stories of her birthplace, would make more sense. The pattern of moves to different homes that we noticed in tracking her addresses, would have been established very early. Though instigated by others in the beginning, it continued throughout her life.

One month after writing to Scotland we had our answer. I could hardly contain my excitement when the Quarriers envelope arrived in my mail box. Amazingly, the contents gave me Grandma's real name—Catherine Walls Scott. We had found her!

Called Katie by her parents, she was born at her grandparents' home near Edinburgh. Her father, a railway stoker described as "ill-doing," left his wife a few years after their child was born. Her mother had custody, and in 1892 left her in the care of Quarriers while she went "to service."

It was four years before Katie's mother reluctantly agreed to relinquish full control to Quarriers. She signed the emigration papers and almost immediately the child left Scotland aboard the *S.S. Siberian*, which left Glasgow May 29, 1896. The children arrived in Brockville on June 9.

One hundred years later, through an incredible set of circumstances, I received a picture of the children who came over on the *S.S. Siberian* in May of 1896. And there she was... my grandmother, Kathleen! Her beautiful little face sprang out at me from the photograph. I couldn't believe it. I thought it would take me forever to find her amongst all the other children, but I recognized her immediately. The family resemblance is stunning.

Having confirmed her identity, I wanted to know more about the tiny child who embarked on a new life as a ten-year-old domestic in rural Canada. I also wanted to know more about her mother. What happened to her after Katie was sent away? Agnes had been so reluctant to give up her only child. What grievious conditions led to this final choice?

The next research phase took nearly three years, and the chase took on a new intensity. Our journey into the past was fascinating. We now know who Grandma's ancestors were, where they lived and how they lived. Actions taken by them in the last century reverberated into this one, and we felt compelled to gather together the bits and pieces and tell the story. All of Katie's grandchildren participated in the process. Memories stimulated other memories, and reviewing events through four perspectives helped a more accurate picture emerge. Where there were gaps in the factual information, we resorted to speculation, based on a new understanding of childhood events.

Going through old letters looking for clues, minutely examining old photos to establish the age of subjects, and exploring memories in conversations with the family was a totally absorbing exercise.

The real story began in 1886....

I

Scottish Connections

Exploring Katie's Origins

*I*t was very puzzling. Our truthful, honest grandmother had lied to us about her past. Dishonesty had always been abhorent in our family and its punishment always severe. To learn that our beloved Grandma had lived under an assumed name was shocking.

Why had she lied? What motivated such an extraordinary action?

Solving the mystery seemed inexplicably urgent to us, even if we did disturb sleeping family secrets. The search for clues quickly became a delicious obsession, and what we found far exceeded anything our active imaginations could have conceived.

Her story began not on July 23, 1889, as we had thought, but three years earlier, when Grandma was born Catherine Walls Scott, not Kathleen Wales Scott. And she was born not in Glasgow or the Isle of Skye but at Woodville, a large estate near Edinburgh, on April 4, 1886. Following Scottish tradition she was named after her maternal grandmother, and was called Katie by her mother.

Katie's mother, Agnes Smith, had married William Scott at Woodville Gardens three weeks before Katie was born. Eighteen-year-old Agnes, the eldest Smith child, had been employed as a domestic servant at Woodville, though the record entry was not clear as to whether or not this meant she worked at the Gardens or at the Mansion House. Catherine Walls Smith stood as witness to her daughter's marriage, performed after Banns, according to the forms of the Church of Scotland. Officiating was William Lockhart, the minister of Colinton Parish for 41 years, who later played a pivotal role in the lives of Agnes and her child Katie.

As our research progressed we kept Agnes' marriage date and Katie's birth date in mind since their proximity immediately signalled that something out of the ordinary had occurred. You will see as we probed deeper and deeper and evidence mounted fact by fact, that it was indeed our first clue in a very complex story.

Agnes' father, George, may have attended the nuptials, but his signature was not included on the marriage document. George Smith was a gardener and domestic servant who had been born in Falkland, Fife, and had been employed at Comrie Castle in 1865 when he married Catherine Walls, a domestic servant in the same county.

All of Agnes' ancestors had lived for many generations in Fife, beginning as early as the 17th century. Family names appear on monument inscriptions in several old Fifeshire cemeteries. They were farmers, labourers, weavers, gardeners, shipmasters, and clerks.

Our Walls ancestors lived mostly in the Saline and Dumfermline part of West Fife, while the Smiths were primarily from the Falkland and Auchtermucty area. Walls family members served as jurors and burgesses in the 18th and 19th centuries, which would suggest some of them lived comfortably, and had resided in the county for several generations. In a Sheriff's Court description found in the *West Fife Family History Society Journal*, jurors were "either special jurors who held heritable property of annual rent of £100 or personal property of £1000—or common jurors, possessors of heritable property of the yearly value of £5 or personal property of £200."

After 150 years of residency, emigration and migration of the families began as employment opportunities declined at home in West Fife. We noticed the deaths of descendants overseas in North America, and in many other parts of Scotland.

Shortly after Agnes was born in 1867, the Smith family moved a few miles south of Culross. Incentive for the move was employment for her father on the large Woodville property. Nine more children were added to the family while they lived there, although not all of the children survived to reach adulthood.

Employed on the estate for at least 25 years, her father was described in the census as a gardener and domestic servant. When her brother George was old enough, he, too, became a gardener at Woodville, and another brother John worked as a papermaker in one of the mills. Other Smith relatives were employed on the property and this suggested that her father may have had more authority than the words gardener-domestic servant would indicate to us. Upon enquiry, I was told by a university authority that the Scottish description, "gardener domestic servant," in connection with a large property at the time, would equate to "estate manager" in modern terms. His responsibilities would also have included access to the Mansion house on a regular basis.

The mansion house, and the staff lodges occupied by the gatekeeper's and gardener's families, were part of the Lands of Woodhall, once an extensive property bordered by the Water of Leith in Colinton Parish, just west of Edinburgh in Midlothian County. The property was rimmed with paper, snuff, corn, and barley mills. By the 1930's the buildings were being converted into schools and religious institutions and were eventually demolished, and the land was cleared and subdivided for suburban housing. The only link now is what remains of a converted gatehouse.

When Agnes was growing up at Woodville, the estate, although diminished from the original Woodhall Lands, was thriving well enough to employ gardeners, a gatekeeper and house servants, and the various mills still provided work for the local people.

Reading about the era, one receives the impression that her family was in a fortunate situation, both economically and socially. Agnes and her siblings would have had advantages not available to most labouring families and one can visualize quiet productive daily activities, with occasional commerce with the owners at the manor house. Hired as a domestic servant when her schooling was complete, Agnes, as the oldest daughter of the Estate Manager, probably felt secure in her environment, and was quite unprepared for the swift change in her circumstances when her father learned she was pregnant at the age of seventeen in the summer of 1885.

The estate was owned by Major General Archibald Alison, Baronet, who inherited the property from his aunt, Mrs. Margaret Alison Burge, after her will was probated in 1882. 1874 and 1875 codicils to this will concerning "The Lands of Woodhall, now called Woodfield or Woodville," had been witnessed by George Smith, gardener (and Katie's grandfather). An ordnance map of 1852 obtained from the Scottish Archives uses the name Woodville for the mansion house, although by 1895, revisions show the name Woodfield being used.

The elderly Mrs. Burge died at the end of December in 1881. She had lived at the Manor with several servants and her niece, Dora Gerard, and both families owned large properties in England and Scotland. Her nephew, Sir Archibald, had two sons and four daughters, and in the spring of 1881 was living at his London home in Kensington, with his wife, Jane Rodger Black, and five of the children. Seven servants and two visitors completed the household. The eldest son, Archibald, was a Sandhurst "gentleman cadet."

The Alison family history dates as far back as 1657 in Midlothian, Perth and Lanark Counties. Three of Sir Archibald's children were born at Ratho, a few miles north of Woodville. One son was born in London and his last two daughters were born in Hampshire, where their father commanded the Aldershot military base.

Major-General Alison inherited his Baronetcy in 1867 from his father Archibald Alison, the Edinburgh historian who wrote *The History of Europe*. In addition to many other military assignments, Major-General Alison had served in the Crimea, and he lost his left arm at "relief in Lucknow." He was also Head of the Intelligence Department from 1878 to 1882, and was Adjutant General from 1888 until his retirement in 1893. Sir Archibald died in 1907.

His eldest son and heir, also named Archibald, lived in London, but maintained his club memberships with United Service at Hurlingham, and at New in Edinburgh. Young Archibald and his brother Randul would have been in their early twenties in 1885, a crucial year in the life of 17-year-old Agnes Smith, the gardener's beautiful daughter.

Agnes

William Scott, described as "ill-doing," left his wife, Agnes, a few years after Katie was born. Agnes was respectably brought up, according to Reverend Lockhart of Colinton Parish, but "made a bad marriage which caused her a great deal of trouble."

The short description probably does not do justice to the difficulties endured by Agnes during her short married life. She came from a stable family, lived comfortably in the same dwelling for many years, and her expectation of marriage, we suspect, was vastly different from what she experienced.

The marriage a few short weeks before the child was born, the early conflict between the two young people, and the physical beauty of the child provoke questions as to Katie's true parentage.

Although William was the legal parent, was he in fact the biological one? The delayed wedding date could suggest an arranged marriage. William was a 26-year-old railway stoker from Edinburgh, who was born June 22, 1859 at Humbie in East Lothian. Colinton was a hub in the railway system, and if he really was was Agnes' lover in 1885, perhaps the young people met in the village at a community social event, or by happenstance in one of the shops.

But if they had been lovers, wouldn't the marriage have taken place when the pregnancy was discovered in the summer of 1885? Was Agnes a reluctant bride? And if William was not Katie's father, why was he chosen to be Agnes' husband?

While pondering over Agnes' situation, I felt the need for more knowledge of the life of young working-class women in the 1880's, and was directed to a book called *The Rise of Respectable Society*, by F.M.L. Thompson, Director of Historical Research at the University of London. It made absorbing reading, and the following was enlightening:

Compulsory education to age 10 in 1876, rose to age 11 in 1893.

Agnes was still classified as a scholar at age 13, which could have meant her family felt education was desirable.

Social networks for working classes were informal, more localized, bound by street, neighbourhood, and workplace.

How then, did Agnes meet and marry William Scott, a railway stoker?

Premarital pregnancies were not necessarily common events for working classes...and were less frequent in the Victorian period.

Sex was not confined to the marriage bed by law or police, but by moral codes backed by religious sanctions. Premarital sex, although probably not normal in the sense of being universal, was not a matter of disgrace among the working classes, so long as it was followed by marriage.

Teenage marriages were extremely uncommon.

After 1871 the mean age of marriages increased to 26.

Most girls who were in service for some part of their lives tended to be slightly older at marriage than other women.

Agnes, a domestic servant, became pregnant at age 17 in the summer of 1885, and was married in the spring of 1886 age 18, three weeks before Katie was born.

Their day started at 5 a.m. and went on until bedtime.

If her free time was so constricted by her duties as a domestic servant, what opportunity did Agnes have to meet young people in her own social milieu or to meet William, who was not likely to have been a part of that milieu?

Young female servants were almost daily faced with seduction by their employers, or the sons of the house.

Did they face the same situation with other servants and/or visitors? Should we be looking at these scenarios as possibilities?

The marriage certificate stated Agnes' usual residence was Woodville. This could mean she was working at the Mansion House, as differentiated from the Woodville Gardens named as the official location of the ceremony. The nomenclature Woodville Gardens was the place of birth for her youngest sister, Ann, in 1889, as well as the death location for her mother, Catherine, but Katie's birth certificate used the name Woodville.

Our Scottish researcher has been asked to submit his opinion on the place names. Woodville appears to be the legitimate name for the Mansion House and the appellation for the three staff outbuildings seems to be Woodville Gardens.

If further evidence surfaces, we may then be confronted with a completely new scenario, of Grandma being born not in the gardener's cottage but in the "big house" where her mother was employed. This could cast further doubt, as well, on our understanding of her biological parentage, which until recently we had believed was the same as her legal ancestry. Her tales of being connected to a long line of Stuarts may prove to be true. Inasmuch as we are skeptical about accepting this possibility, we may eventually have to admit its relevance. DNA tests and photographs would be the ultimate proof, but our story does not warrant such drastic measures.

Three years after Agnes' marriage her mother died of puerperal fever following the birth of her tenth child. Her death must have affected decisions made later for Katie's welfare. A mother's concern and advice for her daughter would not have been available, nor grandparental care for the child when the marriage disintegrated. George Smith continued working on the Woodville estate while caring for their other youngsters. In 1891, two years after his wife's death, seven children were still in residence with him.

Shortly after Agnes' mother died, both of her grandfathers passed away. In their seventies, one had been living in Glasgow with his second wife, and died of a heart attack and the other grandad, who lived in Falkland, died of gangrene. It looks as though relatives may not have been able to offer much in the way of assistance to Agnes or her daughter after William left, and Agnes had full responsibility for Katie's welfare.

Our Scottish researcher could find neither Agnes nor Katie in the Colinton Census Index of 1891. The subsequent census search for all of Scotland also proved negative. Curious, as well, is the fact that a death record could not be found for Agnes, under either her married or maiden name. Since the recording of vital statistics is very thorough in Scotland we were very surprised, and wondered where Agnes could have been living at the time of her death. In England, perhaps?

There was no mention of their difficulties in parish records which makes it seem practically impossible to find out where they might have been living, and with whom. Dr. Lockhart, who ministered Colinton Parish from 1861-1902, would have been consulted by Agnes or the family, as it was he who later prepared the Quarriers orphanage referral, but it is a pity his parish records contained no clues for us.

An October 1892 record entry that Agnes "was paying for her keep while she went into service," indicated to us that Katie and her mother were in separate households. Whether this separation had occurred several years or merely several weeks before her admission to Quarrier Orphan Home is still unknown.

We will continue this search for information on Katie's circumstances after her father left the family, as well as seeking further confirmation of the reasons for her orphanage placement, since many lives were to be affected by Agnes' solution to her problem.

1861–1965

Extract of an entry in a REGISTER of BIRTHS

Registration of Births, Deaths and Marriages (Scotland) Act 1965

No.	1 Name and surname	2 When and where born	3 Sex	4 Name, surname, and rank or profession of father; Name, and maiden surname of mother; Date and place of marriage	5 Signature and qualification of informant, and residence, if out of the house in which the birth occurred	6 When and where registered and signature of registrar
31	Catherine Watt Scott	1886 Tenth April 6 P.M.	F	William Scott Railway Porter (signed) William Scott father	Margaret Scott M.S. Smith Catgate 1886 March 1st	1886 April 1st At Catgate Andrew Landels Spistotal Registrar J.R. Page

The above particulars are extracted from a Register of Births for the Parish _Coelinton_

in the _County_ of _Edinburgh_

Given under the Seal of the General Register Office, New Register House, Edinburgh, on _4 th March 1997_

The above particulars incorporate any subsequent corrections or amendments to the original entry made with the authority of the Registrar General.

This extract is valid only if it has been authenticated by the seal of the General Register Office. If the particulars in the relevant entry in the statutory register have been reproduced by photography, xerography or some other similar process the seal must have been impressed after the reproduction has been made. The General Register Office will authenticate only those reproductions which have been produced by that office.

Warning

It is an offence under section 53(3) of the Registration of Births, Deaths and Marriages (Scotland) Act 1965 for any person to pass as genuine any copy or reproduction of this extract which has not been made by the General Register Office and authenticated by the Seal of that Office.

The document Katie would have treasured, had she known it existed.

II
Quarrier
Orphan

A Label is Acquired...

*K*atie was admitted October 19, 1892 to Quarriers Orphanage, Bridge of Weir, Renfrewshire, Scotland, when she was six years old. "Rev. Wm Lockhart wrote seeking child's admission" stated the report, adding, "Katie seems very self-willed." A tactful comment which perfectly described the Grandma we knew!

The mailing address her mother gave Quarriers was c/o her cousin James Smith at 17 Hozier Street, Partick (Glasgow). Cousin James was not at this address in 1891, but while my brother was doing some census searching, he did find an iron caulker of the same name and approximately the right age, boarding with a family nearby.

The only cousin James we have linked to Agnes thus far was the son of her Uncle William Smith, a loom factory fireman in Falkland. Since he was not living at home with his parents and siblings when the 1891 census was taken, he had probably left home to look for work elsewhere in Scotland.

Did Agnes give her cousin's address to Quarriers because she was living out of Scotland and a Scottish address was required for Katie's orphanage eligibility? Where was Agnes living, if not in Scotland? In England? Where? With whom?

The Quarriers orphan's home had been started in 1871 when William Quarrier rescued three destitute boys from the streets of

Glasgow. His humanitarian work continued to grow, and five years later the Bridge of Weir Village was established a few miles outside Glasgow. When Mr. Quarrier died in 1903, the village had expanded to include 60 cottages and various work buildings.

Although first begun for the rescue of boys from the streets, soon both boys and girls from destitute families in Scotland were being received by the orphanage. The children were often referred by parish ministers, who were aware of the extreme difficulties being encountered by parents trying to house and feed their progeny. *The Quarriers Journal* states:

Classes of children admitted into the Homes—boys and girls deprived of both parents, children of widows or others with no relative able or willing to keep them, from 1-14 years of age, from any part of the country. Destitution is the title for admission....

While they remained at Bridge of Weir, the children attended school, church, and social activities arranged by their caregivers. The were housed in separate group cottages supervised by aides called "parents." As all services were provided within the community there was no need for the children to be outside the village. It was a rather closed world, protected from outside influences and experiences. When Katie first arrived, she must have been overwhelmed by the community. There were so many buildings, so many new faces, and so many new routines for a small child of six.

The number of children living at Bridge of Weir had increased dramatically, housing became critical, and solutions to the problem had been urgent. The idea of emigration became popular, and arrangements were developed whereby groups of the youngsters were sent overseas to Canada. By the time Katie arrived, the yearly emigration of boys and girls was well established.

Katie's four years at the Village, living under its rules, and in its child-oriented community, could not have prepared her very well for emigration to a new country, to live with a family of strangers in the vast countryside of Canada. What enormous adjustments had had to be made by her in these few short years!

Reluctant to give full control of her child to Quarriers, it was four years before Agnes finally signed the permission form for Katie to emigrate. Almost immediately the child left Scotland to become a domestic servant in Canada.

The year 1896 had already been eventful for Katie, starting with New Years Day. All of the children received at least two gifts from donors. "They were sumptuously fed on this holy day, and the days after," noted William Quarrier in his 1897 New Year's letter. Mr. and Mrs. James Burges visited Bridge of Weir with their two young boys, on leave from the Fairknowe Home in Canada. In the spring, there were several magic latern entertainments held. A group of boys were prepared for emigration prior to their April departure. As well, the children were anticipating and preparing for the forthcoming activities to be held on the first Saturday in May. A description of the events was found on a film from the National Archives, and is related here so we have an idea of how Katie spent this day with her mates.

After an early dinner, probably held at the noon hour, the children went out to Play Park with curds, milk, biscuits and fruit. Each house group sat down under flags and banners erected for the occasion. Girls sat on the river side, and the boys sat at the West fence. Two hours of games followed, with races, tug-of-war, and prizes of sweets.

The children were marched back home in file, first up the terrace staircase, then down Faith Avenue, across the new Poultry Farm Bridge, out by the gate of Carsemeadow Farm, and then up the hill to see the new hospital. Photographs were taken of the stream of children on this part of the journey. After visiting the hospital they walked down through the grounds to the main avenue, wending their way back by a side street to the top of the next hill, then home. At this point, more photographs were taken, then the tired children had tea. The photographs on the

National Archives film were not clear enough for reproduction, although one could see the children filing past the buildings.

Mr. Quarrier described it as a happy day, memorable in the history of his work, and I imagine the children found it to be so.

Another item from Mr. Quarrier's letter concerning Katie's group helps us to understand that the preparation for the needs of the emigrating children were not overlooked:

May is always a busy month preparing girls party going to Canada and this one was none of the least. It is not an easy matter to prepare a band of girls with all the nice dresses and other comfortable clothing which they get; but the Lord gave all grace and strength needed to the paupers and ourselves and also the money required. So that all were ready to start when Mr. Burges returned to take the party consisting of 112 girls and 10 little boys, with Mrs. Burges and Miss Quarrier accompanying them and they sailed on 29th May in the good ship Siberian under command of Captain Parkes.

Katie Scott was aboard the *S.S. Siberian*, which left Glasgow for Greenock on May 28th. Her diminutive given name was used on the ship manifest. Katie's picture with the children from the ship, taken after arrival in Brockville, matches feature by feature with our picture of Kathleen Scott at age 22, and confirms the little girl was indeed our future grandma.

The children had been ticketed for passage under contract numbers in groups of nine, selected by age. In Katie's 547 ticket group was Jeannie Ferrar, aunt of the very kind Grace Bruce of Ottawa, who sent me the copy of her treasured 1896 photograph. Grace's father, George Ferrar, age six, was also aboard the *Siberian*, and can be seen with the other boys in the front row of the photograph. Notable in the Brockville Recorder of June 5, 1896 was a letter from William Quarrier, addressed to the editor:

A party of 140 girls...sailed from Glasgow on the 28th inst. All over 8 or 9 years of age are already promised, but we will have a number under that age, and a few as young as 2 or 3 years. Anyone wishing to get a young child should write at once enclosing a minister's reference and railway fare to Fairknowe Home....

The excerpt explains in part how arrangements were made for foster families to take children into their homes, and how young some of the children were. Mr. Quarrier exaggerated the numbers slightly, as *The Quarriers Journal* listed 112 girls and 10 boys aboard the ship. Katie's group was the charge of Mr. Quarrier's son-in-law and daughter, Mr. and Mrs. Burges, and his youngest daughter, whose name, I believe, was Mary Quarrier.

There were two trips by Quarriers orphans to Canada each year. The boys left Scotland in April debarking at Halifax, and the girls' group, which left at the end of May, was able to travel up the ice-free Saint Lawrence river to Quebec City. We tried to find a description of the Siberian's May voyage to Canada in 1896, but were unsuccessful. However, we did find a letter published the previous year, which even though it describes travel by the boys' group, should not be too dissimilar from the girls' voyage in the spring. It gives us a general idea of conditions experienced by the children. From the *Mail*, a Glasgow newspaper, dated May 2, 1895:

Arrival of Children in Canada

Mr. Quarrier has received the following letter from Mr. Alex. Burges, dated Brockville, 13th April—We arrived safely in Brockville, and already more than half the party have gone to their homes. We had a speedy and pleasant passage, with all the comforts for which the Siberian is noted.

We left Greenock about 4 a.m. on the 30th March, and arrived at Moville at 3 p.m. Sea-sickness had hold of a good many on the way over, so the smooth water of the lough was a pleasant change for them. We started out again at 5 p.m., and as we had supper on deck, quite a number were able to do justice to a substantial meal. On Sabbath nearly all hands were sick, still a large number managed to get on deck, although only a very few patronized the dinner table. On Monday we had fine weather, and as we took all the meals on deck, sea-sickness was forgotten, and Irish stew and soup disappeared at an alarming rate.

The fine weather continued all through the voyage, with an exceptional shower, and we only had to take one meal below on account of the rain. All the other meals were taken on deck, and with a greater relish than if taken in the more confined quarters below. As there were few other passengers, the boys had plenty of room for romping, and I'm sure the majority of them were sorry when the time for leaving the ship arrived. Porpoises were seen on several occasions, and also a number of vessels, among them the Sarmatian going east. There was general disappointment at the non-appearance of whales and icebergs. As we steered well south we saw no ice of any kind, and I for one was not disappointed.

On Thursday, April 4th, the boys gave an entertainment which was highly successful, and a very credible collection was taken up at the end for the Sailor's Orphanage. We held most of the services on deck, as we found that some of the boys, even towards the end of the voyage, got a little squeamish if left long below. Captain Parke, who is an old friend, was particularly kind, and did everything in his power to make us comfortable. I cannot speak too highly of the care and devotion bestowed on the party by Mr. Cargill, the chief steward. Indeed, he seemed to make the comfort and welfare of the passengers his one effort, and many a one will bear him in kindly remembrance. His men also were most careful and obliging, and the accommodation provided by the Allan Line Co. was most excellent.

The English-speaking part of our fellow passengers were of a superior class, and the officers and crew were all friendly and kind. "A good captain makes a good crew." Owing to the fine *weather there were no accidents from falls of a serious nature, and Dr. M'Donald soon repaired all damages.*

We reached Halifax before 9 a.m. on Tuesday the 8th, and got away at 12.20 p.m. Mr. Lambkin had two comfortable tourist cars ready for us, and we received every assistance necessary both from Government officials and Canadian Pacific Railways. It rained hard after we left Halifax, but notwithstanding the disagreeable weather we got an enthusiastic reception at Moncton from Rev. Mr. Weeks and friends. A very welcome supply of cakes, pies, etc. were put on board, and the boys left Moncton feeling that they were no longer strangers in a strange land.

On reaching St. John we found that there were several washouts ahead, and had to proceed slowly til daylight. The rain had melted the snow, and the rivers were all in flood and doing a great deal of damage. At M'Adam Junction the Canadian Pacific Railway furnished us with a good meal, and we had the offer of another later on, which we declined as unnecessary. However, we got a good supply of tea, and with the good things furnished by Moncton friends, we fared very well. The Allan Line interpreter, Mr. Helms, accompanied us to Montreal, and was exceedingly attentive and kind and spared no trouble to make the party comfortable. We arrived in Brockville on Thursday at 2.30 p.m., the Ottawa train having been held for an hour at Smith's Falls. Considering the weather and the state of the road we had a very good run, and the C.P.R. Company sent us through as quickly and comfortably as was possible under the circumstances. On both the ship and the train we were treated with the greatest kindnesses and consideration.

The children had a reception at the Baptist church here on Friday night, and now there are not sixty left, and the rest will go to their homes as fast as we can arrange to have them met. The demand for boys is very great, and good boys can always get work. Of this party I can honestly speak in the highest terms, and it would be difficult to select 120 more promising boys, and I am sure neither their native land nor the Orphan Homes of Scotland will ever have reason to feel ashamed of them.

The children usually stayed at the Fairknowe Home in Brockville for a few days while arrangements were completed for their transfer to farming families. On June 11, 1896, the ladies of the Baptist Church entertained the children who had arrived June 9, and the Brockville newspaper reported a good crowd being present, stating, "The exercises were similar to those usually in vogue at such receptions. There are 120 girls in the party, and already homes have been provided for nearly all of them."

Before the children were released to the Canadian farming families, an agreement called an "indenture" was signed by both the receiving family and Quarriers. I'm including the full text of an indenture form, as it makes abundantly clear Mr. Quarrier's expectation of the receiving family. When I read it, I could not help but think that the organization tried to ensure the children were fairly treated, and that its commitment continued after the child's placement. However, as I was later to learn, a written contract did not prevent abuse and/or exploitation by many employers.

I was saddened to learn as well of the accidental shooting of a 14-year-old named Jemima Riddle on the Glassford farm near the village of Glenvale. Shot by an older employee, she had just returned from church, and died within the hour. Jemima had come to Canada on the *S.S. Siberian* with Katie, barely six weeks earlier.

The indenture document uses the term "boy" throughout, but I understand this same form was used for the female children as well.

FILL UP, SIGN AND KEEP THIS HALF
THIS INDENTURE

(Pursuant to Order in Council bearing date of 9th March 1888, authorizing Fairknowe Home to exercise the powers granted under Sec. 29 of Cap. 142, R.SO., 1887),
Made this ____ day of _____, 18___

is entered into between William Quarrier, Fairknowe Home, Brockville, Ontario, Guardian of _____, and

_____
of _____ Township, Con _____ Lot _____
who takes _____
and agrees to give him good clothing and schooling, and treat him as one of the family till able to earn wages, and agrees to give him $____ per month, or $ ____ per annum, with washing and mending for the first year increasing annually; the proposed increase in wages to be submitted for Guardians approval at end of each year.

Also agrees to send the boy to Church and Sunday School regularly; and to Day School one full session yearly according to requirements of Canadian School Law.

The person taking the boy must see that he write to his friends occasionally, and to the Home at least once a year and must immediately notify us of any change of address or in event of sickness. The boy must on no account be transferred to any other person or removed out of the Province without our consent; but can be returned to the Home if he does not suit by sending notice a fortnight beforehand.

We, on our part, reserve the right of removing him on these conditions not being fulfilled, or if we see fit, and the other party to the contract will be held liable for any legal or other expenses incurred if the boy is not sent back when requested by us in writing.

The quantity and quality of clothing must be maintained, and the undersigned of the second part hereby agrees to make up any deficiencies by clothing or money, if the boy is returned or when he is beginning to work for wages.

An accurate account to be kept of money expended for clothing, etc. The account to be made up yearly, a statement sent to the Home, and any balance deposited in P.O. Savings Bank in boy's name.

Railway fare to be paid by person getting the boy and not deducted from his wages if he remains six months. (signed) W. Quarrier per Signed, _____

NOTE: Persons making application for Children should send or bring reference from their Minister. Friends knowing of Children being ill-treated or in unsuitable homes, will confer a favour by communicating with us at Fairknowe Home, Brockville. All such letters will be treated as confidential.

Children sent to the colonies under these British programs became known in Canada as Home Children. With their numbers totalling 100,000 between 1869 and 1930, their descendants now comprise about 11 per cent of the Canadian population.

We understand that the May 1896 contingent of Quarriers Home Children was sent to homes in the Ottawa Valley within a hundred miles of the Brockville receiving centre. But where exactly was our 10-year-old Katie sent to live and work? What was the name of her receiving family?

Examining the Evidence

*K*atie used Scottish expressions frequently throughout her life. When talking with her grandchildren, she often used the phrase, "Dinna fash yersel, lassie," and we remember clearly her repetition of the words "Some hae meat and canna eat, some nae meat that want it. But we hae meat and we can eat, and so the Lord be thankit." Some of my readings suggest this was a Scottish child's grace used at mealtime. We wonder if Grandma cherished the words from a childhood memory of her four years at Quarriers, or heard them later in Canada.

When Grandma told us, as children, her story, we believed she had been placed with her original foster family as a result of the death of her parents in a fire, which we believed had occurred in Canada. We now know that she made up stories about her past, and we have been trying to sift clues as to the name of her receiving family from the names, places, and dates she gave to my father.

Kathleen gave Dad only two addresses concerning her early life. One was for her Uncle, William H. Adams, at 84 O'Connor Street, Ottawa, suggesting the year she joined the family was 1891, the other was 11 Mark Street, Toronto, citing 1911 as the date of habitation. The dates she gave Dad are not accurate since Grandma did not arrive in Canada until June of 1896. She may have moved to Toronto in 1911 but we could only find her name there from 1912 onwards, and cannot confirm when she left Ottawa for Toronto. It seemed logical, however, to continue work on the premise that she lived in the Ottawa area first and later moved to Toronto.

Further investigation showed us that Uncle William's first wife, Charlotte, died in Arnprior. We wondered if Katie had joined the household while they were living in this town. But it seemed unlikely, as the children were usually placed with farming families. We know, from our knowledge of her, that Grandma was always at her most comfortable in farm environments; it must have been childhood experiences which made her feel this way. Neither her life in Ottawa, nor her work in the city of Toronto from her twenties onward, would have provided her with this familiarity of farm life.

About three months after his first wife died, 60-year-old William H. Adams, a General Agent, and 47-year-old Sarah Jean Gordon Kinnaird were married at the home of Gavin Hamilton in Almonte. Shortly thereafter, they moved to Ottawa. Sarah had lived at the Kinnaird family home in Almonte with her brother and sisters, and all the Kinnaird siblings had worked in various capacities in the local textile mills. At the time of her marriage, Sarah and her sister, Annie, operated a Fancy Store.

William had been living in Arnprior with his first wife, Charlotte, and his mother, Jane Bell Adams. His mother died in 1891 at the age of 101. While looking for the newspaper obituary for Jane, we found the papers full of eulogies for another person who had died on the same day—Sir John A. Macdonald. There was no space left to mention Jane's long life in Canada. Five years later William's wife died following complications after a fall.

William's two wives, Charlotte and Sarah, had both been milliners at some point in their lives. Had they known each other through this profession? Is this how Sarah and William had met? Or could her store or the local Presbyterian church have provided the link?

The Presbyterian church played a large role in Sarah's life. All the Kinnairds were baptised in and attended church regularly. Their names appeared on membership rolls and burial plot purchases beginning in 1847, when churches were formalizing their congregational records. Sarah's sister, Annie, married the son of Gavin Hamilton, a Presbyterian Church Elder and Reeve of Ramsay Township. When Annie's husband died in 1896, Annie and the two children went to live with Gavin's family, and, according to the census, were still there in 1901. The families had even closer ties, as Sarah's wedding took place at Gavin's home, and his daughter had been a witness to Annie's earlier marriage in Almonte.

Sarah continued her loyal church membership in Ottawa, and at her death was described as a highly respected, long-time member of Bank Street Presbyterian Church. Her body was later sent home for burial to lie near her family in Auld Kirk Presbyterian Cemetery in Almonte.

Although we cannot confirm the exact date yet, the Adams' move to Ottawa occurred after their marriage and prior to their move to Bay Street where the 1898 directory listed William's employment as an insurance agent. Sarah purchased her O'Connor Street house a year later in July of 1899.

We did not find a child named Catherine, Katie or Kathleen Scott connected with the family, either through census, city directories, or church records from 1896 to 1902. Where was she? Perhaps living on a farm near Ottawa?

Farmers usually picked the biggest and strongest children for heavy farm work. The smaller children were domestics. At age 10, tiny Katie would have been categorized as a domestic servant. At age 10! Considered cheap labour, the children carried a stigma for the rest of their lives. The prevailing attitude was that these children, many who were merely economically deprived, were "depraved."

David Lorente, of Heritage Renfrew explains, "Home Children do not talk of their past, perhaps because of the stigma that most felt was attached to them...Some Home Children perceived themselves as 'discards' or rejects. It was widely held that mental, physical, and moral deficiencies were equated with the lower clases of society. It was also held that the defects were inherited."

Since this attitude prevailed throughout Canada, abuses occurred, although mistreatment of the children was often neither observed, reported nor alleviated. Pressure began to mount as well by eugenicists, who bemoaned the poor control of these "degenerate children," and who opined they might "contaminate Canadian blood lines." But eventually word began to spread by citizens concerned about the conditions endured by the children. Eloquent letters were received by the Canadian Government sent both by neighbours and the children themselves.

The Quarriers organization appears to have made more thorough preparations in their child selection process for emigration, as well as in their supervisory methods once the children arrived in Canada. Abuses still occurred, unfortunately, but it seems their methods were to solve the problems in house, and few documented cases are available for research.

Before the end of each year, it was routine for Mr. Quarrier to compose greetings in the form of a newsletter describing the events of the year. The year 1896 was no exception, and part of the New Year's Letter dated 1897 addressed to "Our Children and Friends in Canada" reads as follows:

Now I will close with a word of advice, and would ask you to be willing and obedient to those with whom you are placed, not seeking your own will, but doing the will of God from your heart. In all perplexity where human wisdom and experience are required, you should consult with Mr. and Mrs. Burges, who are your true friends, also be sure to write home to your mother if she is still alive. I am often told that the letters sent by them are not answered, or that you have never written.

Now I commend you to the care of our Heavenly Father and to the word of his Grace, which is able to keep you from falling, and I pray that each one of you, my dear children may be a true follower of Him who gave Himself for you....

This portion of the newsletter solidified my impression that Quarriers made efforts to remain in touch with the children placed in Canada, and that religion played a prominent role in their teachings. A jarring note, to me, however, is the concern expressed about letters to and from mothers. Did the children truly receive letters sent by their mothers? Were letters from children actually posted and did all employers make it possible for the children to send and receive letters?

According to Gillian Wagner's book *Children of the Empire*, an act was passed in 1897, "to regulate immigration into Ontario of Certain Classes of Children, which, it was hoped, would mollify public opinion. Under the Act, the work of each agency was to be inspected 4 times a year. Careful supervision over the children was to be maintained until they attained 18 years of age. It was further provided that all agencies were to maintain proper homes for the reception of the children and for their shelter in time of need."

One National Archives film notes a letter sent from Lynwode Peirera, Assistant Secretary of the Department of the Interior in Ottawa to immigration agents. Dated January 21, 1898, it states, "Sir, I am decried by the Superintendent of Immigration to request you to immediately commence inspection of immigrant children." A list of agencies, including Quarriers, follows the text of the letter.

Because Mr. Quarrier objected to the these actions, immigration from Bridge of Weir ceased in the spring of 1898, and did not resume until sometime after his death in 1903. However, the staff at Fairknowe continued services for the children already placed with families in Canada.

Indenture

Kathleen had told us, her grandchildren, she was abused as a child. Her story was that she was removed from a foster home about age 12, and placed with a second family until she reached age 16. A careful examination of the Quarriers report numbers in Katie's file (trying to decode their numbering system) would lead me to believe that her dating of this removal is true. Using her actual birth date in 1886 rather than the fictitious 1889 that we knew, we translated the code as follows:

1896 May 29 To Canada = Aboard *S.S. Siberian*

L 22/96. = Letter to Scotland 1896 (age 10)

R 15/31. = Report 1896

63/34a-64/43 12/60, 5/87, 14/90e, R 6/98. = Reports 1898 (In June of 1898, Katie was 12 years old)

1/3/02 Letter R 20/10 from Katie. = A report at the end of her indenture in 1902, plus a letter from Katie to Scotland (In 1902, Katie was 16)

Something very unusual was happening in Katie's life for so many reports to have been written in 1898. A yearly visit was normal, but this many reports would point to problems being encountered by the child. Katie was probably removed from her first foster family in the summer of 1898.

We continue the story with events occurring in Ottawa....

Eight months after the flurry of reports on Katie, a female child was born in Ottawa and was adopted by Sarah and

44

William Adams. A few months later Sarah (not her husband) purchased the O'Connor Street house from its long-time owners, the Huband family.

On July 11, 1900 the child, called Florence Bell Adams, was baptized in Bank Street Presbyterian Church, giving the place of birth as O'Connor Street—no house number was given. I noticed on the record that the two words were placed at one edge of the column, with space left by the recorder, perhaps for later insertion of the house number, or to indicate an anomaly. The name of the birth mother was never found and the omission seems to suggest secrecy surrounding an illegitimate birth.

I think there may be a connection between Katie's story and these events. Katie was a extraordinarily beautiful child, and it is not difficult to imagine her innocence and trust being betrayed. We have also learned that Sarah Adams, whom Grandma called Aunt Sarah, was extraordinarily kind to young people, and may have been her rescuer in 1898. The youngster may have had to face adult problems, and could have been one of the cases described in the National Archives Home Children files as "A Case of Seduction." Nowadays, we recognize this as "rape." Pregnancy of the very young, vulnerable Home Children was not all that unusual.

The *St. Catharines Daily Times* noted in 1875, "One of Miss Rye's girls—herself a mere child appearing about 12 or 13 has been delivered of an infant," and as Gillian Wagner wrote in *Children of the Empire*, "Annie McMaster had a child by the son of her master." One yearly, unconfirmed report stated that sixteen Home Children had illegitimate babies. When the girls tried to complain about sexual harassment, they were themselves blamed for the incidents. They were at the mercy of their aggressors.

The 1901 Ottawa Census shows Sarah Adams as a lodging housekeeper, and her husband, William, as a carpenter, a change from his employment in 1899 as an insurance agent. This could intimate that Sarah may have recently shouldered responsibility for the financial security of the family. No child of Katie Scott's name or age is registered with the family, nor a person called Ida Adams, whose role in this story begins later on in 1909. Besides Sarah and William, the name of Florence, their adopted daughter is there, as well as a 22-year-old Quebec-born lodger called Mary Hamilton. A crossed-out entry, on which we could still see the name of Bella Halpenny, described her as a lodger, although no age was entered for Bella, and we do not yet know the role she may have played in our story.

Katie was not at Fairknowe Home in 1901, either. Only one child, Grace Ronald from the *S.S. Siberian* group of June 1896, was resident on the census date, working in the Home as a domestic. Alexandra Burges, a widow, was Manager, assisted by Ann M. Burges, Matron, and Winnifred E. Burges, Nurse. I was struck by the spelling similarity in the names "Burges" and that of "Burge" of Woodville Manor. But where was Grandma?

As we continued searching for answers on Katie's whereabouts, there were several points we kept in mind. One, she worked on a farm. Two, she was abused during her first placement and was situated at a second. Three, her indenture ended in 1902 when she reached sixteen and was released to find her own way in the world. And four, she knew the Adams family and their ten-year (1899-1910) O'Connor street address in Ottawa.

Lacking confirmatory documentation for this period, logic suggests she lived with them sometime between 1902 and 1910, although the birth of the child Florence Bell in 1899 must not be overlooked, nor the fact that Grandma used the date 1891 as the year she joined the family. Every tiny clue had relevance, either pointing us in the right direction towards the truth, or containing a germ of truth....

The story Kathleen told Dad—that she was born in Scotland July 23, 1889, and was the daughter of Robert and Agnes Wales Scott, bears little relation to the real facts. But she may have had no knowledge of the real facts! As Margaret Humphreys wrote in *Empty Cradles*, "These people had absolutely no evidence of when they were born, apart from childhood recollections...

46

Child migrants had been outrageously deceived. They don't know they're celebrating [their birthdays on] the wrong date."

Many children were told that their parents had died. But as Gillian Wagner commented in *Children of the Empire*, "Less than one third of the children admitted to the Homes were total orphans or completely destitute...."

One contributor to Kenneth Bagnall's book, *The Little Immigrants*, admitted that, "Here in Canada there are still people who would look down their noses at anyone raised in a Home. That is why I concoct nice stories for inquisitive friends who wonder how I came out here. Much of it I never told my husband."

The same book relates the story of one shrewd girl who described her situation as such: "'doption Sir, is when folks get a girl without wages."

Later in life, some home children were even refused inheritances, government assistance, or even pension income, when they could not provide proof of birth.

We were curious to know how Grandma chose the particular names and dates she gave to us. As well, research into her story of having connections to the Stuart family name, and as she constantly reminded us, "was spelled the same as Bonnie Prince Charlie," has not yet proven to be true, though we checked back many generations. We wondered how this name also became part of Katie's legend. Were the names borrowed from people she knew as a child? Our second challenge was to discover where she lived on first coming to Canada.

Putting the two together, we thought about the possibilities: the names of places, and names of people she knew. None of Katie's relatives were named Wales. We found that there were many Wales families living in the Addington-Frontenac area, north of Kingston. But since it seemed such a huge project to start looking for a connection to Grandma using their surname, my research began with the names of places.

Working on this theory, I discovered a small farming community town named Wales a few miles from Cornwall. It was a

Scottish settlement whose area roads in 1997 still reflected its origins. Although the town no longer exists, there is a new subdivision named Wales Village, south of the highway 401 access, off Wales Road. A Stuart family still lives on property just south of the Wales Village subdivision.

The Gazetteer of 1908 described Wales, Ontario, as, "a post village in Stormont County, Ontario, one mile from the St. Lawrence River and a station on the G.T.R., ten miles west of Cornwall. It has two churches (Episcopal and Presbyterian) two stores, one hotel, one bank (Molsons) besides telegraph and express offices—pop. 250." It is interesting to note that Wales is just north of Dickinson's Landing in Osnabruck Township, with easy railway connections to Ottawa.

I counted seven Stuart families owning property in Osnabruck Township in the 1885-86 Directory of the area. Of particular interest was Robert Stuart, the Postmaster at Woodlands, who lived about a mile west of the town of Wales in the same township. Holding this position from the opening of the post office in 1864, until its closing in 1909, Robert no doubt knew several generations of every family in the area. A Presbyterian Scot, he and his wife, Agnes, had two daughters born in Ontario. His youngest daughter had a birth date of July 23.

The similarities between the daughter's birth date, the parent's given names, and Grandma's use of these names were quite intriguing. Is it possible she may have known the family?

It seems logical that a child writing letters to Scotland would know the local postmaster and his family. Could the Stuarts have taken an interest in Katie? Could Katie have borrowed the birth date of another teenager she knew and liked? Is this the significance of her choice of July 23, 1889 as her birthday? And the choice of the names Robert and Agnes for her parents?

Using this clue, and the information that most of the May 1896 Home Children had been placed on farms in the Ottawa Valley, I spent an entire summer examining every township census in Eastern Ontario, from Brockville east to the Ontario-Quebec border and as far north as Renfrew county, looking for a child who might be Grandma. Finally, I found one, named Catherine, who was the "adopted" daughter of an elderly couple living on a farm a mile or so from Wales. She had been born in Scotland in 1886 and the year of immigration given in the census was an approximate match with Grandma's. She could be our Katie!

Unfortunately, all early records for the orphaned children were destroyed when the Quarriers Canadian program ceased in 1930. We examined filmed parish records that same summer, hoping to find a Katie or Catherine Scott on a Presbyterian communion or membership list, but the entries were mostly for births, marriages and deaths. We have not yet found any other existing sources for children who may have attended church services, although we have heard that a few school census records may have survived. This part of the research will continue, as we search for other sources to confirm Katie's two farm assignments.

The last written communication with Quarriers in Scotland is a letter from Katie dated March 1, 1902. The record did not stipulate if the letter was addressed to Agnes or to the association. Katie may have sent letters through Quarriers for her mother, but we do not know whether Agnes would have received them.

My impression is that most agencies wished for a clean break between the families overseas and the children in Canada. I have read many letters from Home children imploring placement agencies to give news of families and siblings. Whether the agencies ever gratified this wish is unknown. My research suggests not, since similar requests were received year after year, with the words "its been 3 years and I haven't heard," or "Where is my brother (or sister), I am looking for him," or "I went to ____ she's not there, where is she?"

Quarriers seemed to have had different policies, though. One letter received by Quarriers and printed in the *Bridge of Weir* publication of June 9, 1896, reads: "I will close with my best wishes to yourself, Mrs. Quarrier and Frank. P.S. I enclose a letter to my mother, please give it to her. A.Y."

Katie reached age 16 on April 4, 1902, and her indenture was over. Did she leave the farm, and head for the nearest city, Ottawa? Was it at this point the spelling of her name was revised? What prompted her choice—Kathleen Wales Scott rather than Catherine Walls Scott? And the birth date of July 23, 1889 instead of April 4, 1886? Since she used the name Catherine Scott on mother's marriage registration, we know that she knew her real name. Her use of "Kathleen Wales" could not have been simply a spelling mistake. Once again, Gillian Wagner sheds some light on this discrepancy. She writes of one former Home Child: "There is some suggestion that Sarah had deliberately changed her name, something that was done by a fair number of children who wished to sever all connection with the homes."

On September 18, 1902, Florence Bell Adams, Sarah's adopted child, died of scarlet fever, and William reported it to the Registrar, declaring the child's age as three years, seven months and four days. This would make her birth February 14, 1899, not May 14, 1899 as reported by Sarah on the 1901 census. A search through Ontario Vital Statistics records for a female child born on either of these dates in Ottawa has not proved fruitful.

But why had Sarah felt it necessary to give an inaccurate birth date on the census? Her own age and birth date were inaccurate on the census as well. And why did Sarah not report the death? Was she distraught? She normally took care of these matters. Considering the fact that Sarah had lost five sisters to disease, the death of another child may have affected her greatly. Since we have confirmed that William Adams always accurately reported information for census purposes, we plan to use his version of Florence's birth date in this story.

We next tried to confirm Katie's whereabouts by exploring city directories. There was only one Kate Scott listed in Ottawa, in 1903, but she had been living with her parents at the same address in the 1891 census, before our Katie came to Canada. There was no listing for a Kathleen Scott.

Double-checking, I asked the Ottawa City Archives to look for a Catherine Scott for the years 1902 to 1912. On June 13, 1997, the reply came through. There was only one. Catherine Scott, widow of William, in the 1904 directory, and therefore, not our Catherine. They were unable to locate a Catherine Scott in any Ottawa city directory prior to, or after, 1904.

There were no Toronto Directory listings for Kathleen Scott until 1912. But Katie had been earning her living since age 16 and lived in Ottawa or Toronto between 1902 and 1912. Not finding her address under either name over a ten year period was indeed puzzling. Ten years is a long time. What was happening to her in those important youthful years?

An old, very faded (and unusable) family photograph depicts a beautiful, smiling Kathleen, standing in a field near a lake. Smiling at the camera, she is wearing a checked dress with white collar and cuffs. This is the only time I have seen her with her hair parted on the side, rather than in the centre, even though it appears to be long, and wound into a bun at the nape of her neck. By the time she was 25, she was using a more severe hair style. We estimate the picture was taken around 1906, when Katie was about 20 years old.

IV
Beloved Daughter

William Adams, 'Aunt' Sarah's husband, had a stroke in the spring of 1909 and was bedridden for six months. That same summer, purportedly, Mother was born in Toronto. According to the 1967 Late Attestation Mother filed, her birth occurred in Toronto on June 15, 1909, though we could find no confirmation that Grandma was living in Toronto that year.

Grandma had told Dad her Toronto address in 1911 was 11 Mark Street. One could speculate that her first Toronto address was well remembered, when she lived as a boarder with her friends Hector and Margaret MacDougall. We know that the MacDougalls lived in Toronto starting in 1909, but Grandma's name did not appear in a city directory until 1912. If Grandma was living in the city in 1909 why was there this mysterious gap of three years?

We also do not have proof from an alternate source that 1909 was Mother's year of birth. No 1909 birth registration was filed. We have only her word. There was no birth certificate for her amongst the family papers. Dad had specifically described the documents contained in a brown envelope, on the outside of the envelope. Mother's birth certificate was missing. Who would have removed it? And why? Adding to the mystery is an incident recalled by one of the grandchildren, which will be revealed later on in this story.

Grandma always maintained that Norman Scott was her husband. The only Norman Scott who seemed a likely candidate lived in Ottawa near Aunt Sarah. The son of a wealthy mill owner, he may have been the child's father, but we have, as yet, found no marriage record. Indeed, Mother's 1928 marriage registration described the father of the bride as "not known." Grandma may have simply borrowed his name for her legend.

'Uncle William' Adams died in November of 1909, and his sole surviving daughter was named Ida Adams. 'Aunt Sarah' would have given these details to the Ottawa newspaper, since she was the one who reported his death to the Registrar's Office. But who was Ida? Ida continued to live with Sarah until the end of 1911, working at the Bate & Co. Grocery Store.

There was no 1910 Ottawa directory entry for Sarah or Ida, which seems significant, as Sarah had an entry every year before and after 1910, until her death in 1930.

On February 13, 1911, Sarah purchased a newly built house in the suburbs, and Ida and Sarah moved to Gordon Street, near Dow's Lake. The first house had been built in 1906, and for a time was the only house on the street. Sarah's house was built four years later. What was the motivation behind the purchase of the new house in a country setting? There were only a few houses on the street, it was surrounded by fields, far distant from the centre of the city where Sarah was used to living. Was there a child in the household that provided impetus for this purchase and move?

I was beginning to wonder if Ida and Kathleen were the same person. There is no evidence to suggest that a daughter was ever born to William and his first wife Charlotte—not in the Census, in city directories, nor in Ontario vital statistics records from 1869-1900. Nor could we find a child born to William and his second wife, Sarah, using the same research sources. One fact remains constant, though: Grandma knew the Adams family before 1911, as she had given their name and O'Connor Street address to Dad.

Ida continued to live with Sarah, working at the same grocery store. The last directory entry for her, in 1912, did not list any employment. Since occupation was normally included in the data, we assume Ida was not working. The O'Connor street house was being rented for use as a Chinese laundry.

No further information on Ida was found—no birth, no marriage, no death. We never did find anything to show William Adams was her blood connection, nor did Ida's name ever appear in any Census with the family. When we tried to check assessment rolls, which in 1912 included numbers of family members, we discovered the rolls for their ward had been burned in a fire. Again we drew a blank.

The mystery deepened, as I imagined possiblilities. Could the two names have belonged to only one person? Why have no documents have been found to confirm their separate identities? Nudging me is the fact Grandma used her real name Catherine Scott only once, when Mum and Dad were married in 1928. What would be easier than using the Adams name while she lived with them? Or was Ida another adoptee absorbed into the family for a few years?

The name, Mrs. Kathleen Scott, appeared for the first time in the 1912 Toronto Directory living at the 11 Mark Street home of Hector McDougall, a painter. No occupation was listed for Mrs. Scott.

If we were working on the supposition of the two names applying to one person, could Kathleen have used one name in Ottawa in December 1911, and a new one in Toronto after moving away from Ottawa in early January 1912? Checking this possibility, we found out that information for Ottawa Directories was submitted in late December prior to publication the following summer. Submissions for the Toronto Directory, it has been suggested to me, were gathered after the beginning of the year.

It therefore seemed possible for a person to be listed in two different cities in the same year. And so the two separate threads of the story begin to appear. The checkered life of the tiny Scottish child, Katie, and the mystery surrounding her child, our mother Dorothy.

 We have a picture of Mother in an exquisite lace and embroidered dress, about age two, holding a china doll wearing the same beautiful handmade attire. The background appears to be a studio setting, and the elaborately trimmed garments appear to be baptismal gowns. Her hair is carefully coiffed, but there is a glum expression on her face. The doll, named Isobel, was carefully preserved for over 60 years, and Mother allowed us to admire her only on special occasions. ("Look, but don't touch!" we were admonished.) Unfortunately, Isobel was stolen during a robbery at our parents's home in the Eastern Townships. Mother was devastated.

Grandma had told Dad her child was baptised at home when she was between two and three years old by a Rev. Wilson, a Presbyterian. Why was she not more specific? Mothers usually know the exact age at which their children are baptised, especially when there is only one child, and a beautiful studio photo is taken to mark the event.

Which city was the locale for the baptism? There was no evidence of a minister named Wilson in Grandma's parish during the designated time period, nor for the baptism of her child in Toronto Presbyterian or Methodist records. Mother did attend Sunday School at Trinity Methodist, as we have her signed booklet in family archives. The handwriting was back-slanted and mature, the signature of a teenager, not an elementary school child. I found out later that she attended Trinity church while living with a Toronto family between 1921 and 1927. Membership and Communion records no longer exist to enable us to check when she joined the congregation.

There was a William A. Wilson at the Methodist Church in Ottawa from the summer of 1910 to the summer of 1912. Although he found no entry for Mum under the name Scott or Adams in the church records, the Archivist told me that the minister could have neglected to register a home baptism. There were no membership or Sunday School records available to check for her name, but until we learn to the contrary, the possibility exists that Dorothy lived in Ottawa as a youngster.

My sister recalled overhearing our mother talking with friends one day about "the glebe." Feeling slightly guilty for eavesdropping, the youngster didn't ask, but always wondered what the strange words meant. When we were deep into Ottawa research we realized Aunt Sarah lived in "The Glebe" area. Astonished, my sister remembered where she had first heard these words. We then postulated that if Mother had always lived in Toronto, it was not likely she knew the name of this particular district. Ergo, Ottawa played a role in her life.

There is a beautiful family picture of Grandma with the words "Mrs. Scott, age 22," on the back. She is standing by a big tree, unsmiling, facing the camera, grass at her feet, wearing a middy blouse and a long dark skirt. The background shows a country setting, with big trees, long grass, and slender pines.

Grandma's features in this picture, as well as her expression, match exactly with those of the 10-year-old child who came to Canada on the *S.S. Siberian* in May of 1896. We do not know which birth year was used to date the photograph. The subject looks older than 22 to me. Her serious expression and air of maturity would lend credence to her age as 25. In which case, the picture could have been taken in 1911 at 'Aunt Sarah's' new home, after Dorothy was born.

Was there indeed a real person separate from Kathleen named Ida Adams? I find this hard to believe, since I can find records for everyone else, but not for Ida.

Here's my theory:

Katie was abused in the spring of 1898 and was removed from the farm. Eight months later, in February of 1899, a baby was born at an O'Connor street address. Sarah was made aware of the problem through her church connections, and arrangements were made for Sarah to adopt the newborn. Sarah purchased her O'Connor street house in the July of 1899 and the baby was baptized in the Presbyterian church the next summer.

It was probably decided that young Katie should complete her indenture, and she was placed on another Ontario farm until she reached age 16. The contract obligations completed in 1902, she was released. Since the youngster had few options, she returned to Ottawa. Tragically, the child named Florence Bell Adams died unexpectedly of scarlet fever a few months later.

Katie continued to live with the Adams and attended school where she met Norman Scott. When the Adams encountered financial difficulties as a result of William's poor health, Katie left school and began working in a grocery store.

Sometime after Katie's pregnancy with Dorothy became evident, William had another stroke and died. Sarah rented her house and took Katie away. After the birth, it was decided that a house would be purchased on the outskirts of Ottawa, away from the centre of the city, but close enough for Sarah to attend her church.

Unemployment was high in Ottawa and Katie was forced to seek employment elsewhere when her child was still very young. Uncertain of her future, she left her child with Sarah, visiting Ottawa when finances permitted. When Sarah became too old and feeble to continue her care, the child went to join her mother in Toronto.

Of course, my imagination may be working overtime. Grandma's use of the word "abuse" in her conversations with us, though, was very unusual for the 1950's. Her hints about her past experiences, her harsh assessment of certain conduct and her expressions of much sadness would be more understandable as we look back with the benefit of time and distance. We recollect her anger, her attitude towards trivial hardships, her calm competence in coping with family problems, and her life of sheer hard work. These rememberances, considered together with her continual loving attention to all children and the mounting evidence, make it a theory we have to test.

The War Years

In January 1914, within four days of each other, Aunt Sarah's brother John Kinnaird died of heart failure in Almonte, and her dear sister Annie, who had been living near her in Ottawa, died of peritonitis from a perforated ulcer.

Annie Kinnaird Hamilton and her two daughters, Margaret and Evelyn Sara, had left Almonte in 1907 to live in Ottawa. After two years residence at Albert street, they moved to Lyon, and when the girls were old enough they became stenos for local firms. Annie's great-granddaughter, who now lives in the Toronto area, believes the girls lived with their Aunt Sarah for a time after their mother died in 1914.

Sometime prior to the collection of information for the city directory in 1915, Kathleen Scott, a domestic worker, was living as a boarder at Sumach Street in Toronto. Across the street lived her friends Hector and Margaret MacDougall, with whom Grandma had lived on Mark Street in 1912.

Hector joined the 204th Battalion of the Canadian Expeditionary Force at the beginning of April 1916, and was discharged as medically unfit in October. He had been transferred from the 204th to Casualties on August 29, 1916, and died three years later in Spadina Hospital. His pay records are headed "Overseas Contingent," but it is not yet clear to me if he did in fact go overseas and was wounded in France. Margaret regularly received his army payment at their home on Sumach Street.

In 1916, a Kathleen Scott was working as a saleslady at Woolworths in downtown Toronto, while living at the YWCA on Patrick Street. There is a small picture of Mother taken about this time, when she was five or six years old, wearing matching handmade hat and coat, with a purse on a chain around her neck. Long stockings and gloves complete the stylish outfit. We see extensive lawn, a broad road and wooden sidewalk in the foreground. In the background, bushes and trees. She is smiling slightly, as one can see by carefully examining her face under the broad brimmed hat. This picture reinforces my earlier impression that Kathleen's daughter was living in a comfortable, middle class household, and could not have been living at the YWCA with her mother.

In the fall of 1998 my sister found a tiny gold locket amongst some bits of jewellery inherited from mother. It has the name Dorothy on one side and June 15, 1914 on the other. Inside is a picture of Grandma on the right and Mother as a little girl on the left. We felt the locket was a curious gift for so young a child, unless, as we suspect, they did not live in the same city and it was given as a remembrance by her mother, visiting on her birthday.

If Mother's birth year was indeed 1909, she would have begun elementary school about 1914 or 1915. She never spoke of her life prior to High School, and we wonder why. The total lack of information about this period of her life in the family archives arouses our curiosity, and stimulates conjecture about her circumstances and experiences in her formative years. Mother told us she had had rheumatic fever as a child, but we have no idea what year she was ill, or who took care of her while her mother Kathleen was working. She always maintained that the disease weakened her heart, and it seemed to cause her some trouble later on.

Grandma had a medal with two bars of six months service each, awarded by the Imperial Munitions Board in the First World War for women workers. This medal is confirmation that Kathleen worked in a munitions factory for at least one year during the First World War. If the above named addresses are correct, she would have to have gone to this work in 1914 or 1917. The later year is more likely, as the Government would not have been prepared at the beginning of 1914 to organize and build the factories. Both the medal, and the gold wedding band Kathleen wore, were made by Ellis Bros. of Toronto. The firm was established in 1836 and amalgamated with Henry Birks Ltd. in 1934. There was no Ellis branch office in Ottawa, which would suggest that the items were only available in Toronto. Both ring and medal are treasured family possessions.

My theory that Grandma's entry into munitions work occurred around 1917 is supported by the book *Marching to Armageddon 1914-1918, Canadians and the Great War*. Desmond Morton and J. L. Granatstein describe how a Shell Committee was organized in September 1914, with contracts awarded by May 1915 to 250 firms across Canada. An Imperial Munitions Board was established in December 1915, run by Joseph Wesley Flavelle, a Toronto millionaire.

A strike of the workers in 1916 was broken by the passing of the War Measures Act. This Act was also used to suppress any "reports of discontent, bad working conditions, or sexual

61

assaults on women munitions workers." By 1917, 30,000 women of a total quarter million workers were employed in 600 factories. Production was worth two million dollars a day. Some of the these firms were British Explosives at Renfrew and Trenton; Canadian Explosives at Nobel (near Parry Sound and built in 1917); British Acetone at the Gooderham and Worts Distillery, Canada Cement, Northern Electric, all in Toronto; and British Forgings located at Ashbridge Bay, near Toronto.

The work in the factories was hard and very dangerous. The advertisements stated that girls under 18 "need not apply," although many did, and gave a false birth year. Slogans urged women to "do their bit," and a popular song at the time was "Ammunition Girl." They wore khaki or blue overalls and gloves to work the assembly line, and the "tough" women in blue overalls were described as "blue devils." One of the processes was feeding cordite, looking like brown sugar, into a press. The resulting spaghetti-like material was then batched by the workers, who called it "dope." Wages were low and everyone was exposed to toxic materials. A worker was fired if found carrying matches, no hair could be exposed while on duty and accidents were frequent. Most were deathly afraid of lightning storms, when the buildings would shake, and could set off the raw explosives.

At first, all supervisory personnel were male. Resenting the entrance of women into their domain, their treatment of them was less than exemplary; in small and large ways it was made clear to the women that their presence was not desired. A lack of cooperation, undeserved complaints to management, incorrect instructions to staff, verbal and physical abuse all played a part in the campaign to show women their place was at home, not in a munitions factory. The women found ways to deal with the additional stress placed upon them, and became loyal, good workers. Eventually the women were able to assume supervisory positions in spite of the additional difficulties with which they had to contend. Employers recognized their value as production increased in the plants.

A Scottish novel describes similar conditions where women workers were distrusted, and the men resentful of their presence. It took time for them to be accepted by their male counterparts. The women also handled raw explosive materials, such as TNT and phosphorus (a deadly poison). Toluene made their skin turn yellow as it became stored in their fatty tissue, and earned them the name "canaries." An automatic hopper poured explosives into empty shell casings, which operatives tamped down to eliminate air spaces. The special gloves used by them were clumsy and increased the danger of spill, when the casings became slippery. Some women disobeyed the rules and neglected this small safety precaution. Tiny fragments of phosphorus came in contact with their skin, causing burns which quickly turned septic. Some of these septic sores turned cancerous, and the women died.

Grandma worked for at least a 12-month period, and possibly more, in these difficult factory conditions, and we've often wondered if her health problems in middle age were a legacy arising from poor diet as a youngster in combination with long exposure to the toxic munitions components.

Decades later, a National Film Board production, *And We Knew How to Dance*, sketched the experiences of women who voluntarily joined the war effort as ambulance drivers, nursing sisters, farm hands, and munition workers. I was very impressed by the personal interviews with survivors, which illuminated the camaraderie they had developed with their co-workers, and how it reinforced their determination to perform these dangerous wartime tasks.

Twists and Turns

It has been said that there is no single truth—we may uncover layers, but not solve the mystery. And so it seemed, as we followed the twists and turns of our mother's puzzling early life.

Our next evidence was a picture of her, about age seven, embracing a younger child with short dark hair. Both children appear to be wearing party dresses. Once again, we see a very well dressed Dorothy. Her garment is imaginatively designed and the fabric exquisite. The background where the children are standing appears to be a field, with bushes and trees in the distance. I doubt Kathleen had the full care of her daughter at this time, and suggest they were not living in the same household during the First World War.

On the back of a matte picture of Mother, about age nine, sitting on a cushion are the words, "Mrs. Scott 120 Crescent Road #2254 1 frame 3/8 in of gold $1.00 Monday night her own glass." Frederick Gooch was head of household, and here again Grandma probably was the housekeeper. (Amazingly my two brothers rented an apartment just one block from this address many years later!) It is a lovely picture of Dorothy, sitting on a flowered cushion placed on the grass, with a background of bushes. Wearing a beautifully tailored and lace handmade dress, she shows a smiling healthy face. Her long curly hair is tied with a ribbon. A glossy small-sized shot of the same scene has the

words "Mrs. Scott, small frame" on the reverse side. Where was this picture taken? And when? About 1918?

I inherited the two photographs after Grandma died. When I removed the two frames recently, I was able to see the writing on the back showing her home address. I also remember seeing a picture of Grandma taken the same day, sitting with her daughter on a vivid, flower-print cushion. The pictures could have been taken while they were visiting together in the summer.

Although few in number, the pictures I inherited show an exquisitely dressed child, well cared for and healthy. The clothes were all handmade, and beautifully tailored. Grandma could mend, but she was a knitter, not a seamstress. Sarah had grown up in the cloth trade, was a milliner, and at one time had her own "fancy store" with her sister Annie as assistant, where we believe they would have sold fabrics and sewing notions. Was Aunt Sarah instrumental in the development of the lovely clothing Dorothy wore?

Is our theory valid, then, that Aunt Sarah cared for the young child in Ottawa while her mother worked in Toronto? Evidence seems to suggest that Dorothy joined her mother after the war, when she was about 11. Sarah may have been lonely all by herself in the suburbs as the War ended, since she asked Bessie Louise Cook, a stenographer for J.C. Whyte & Son, to share her house. Sarah was by then about 70 years old.

At about 12 years old, Mother was photographed again, about 1920 this time, standing in a country setting, holding the collar of a large dog. She looks like a healthy-looking, well-nourished girl, wearing horn-rimmed glasses, a charming handmade garment, with matching stockings and shoes. Was this picture also taken near Aunt Sarah's house in Ottawa? Once again we are struck by the disparity between the living circumstances of Dorothy and those of her mother, Kathleen.

In 1920, Mrs. Kathleen Scott lived at McKenzie Street, near to the Danforth Road, where Mr. John A. Ross was head of household. Confirming this information 50 years later was one of our former neighbours and a dear friend, who remembered

Grandma's descriptions of taking strolls along the Danforth. These conversations took place in the 1940's on our front lawn, while Grandma was taking a break between household chores. Once again Kathleen had come to help her daughter cope with the responsibilities of her large family. Evidently, everyone in the neighbourhood knew Mother was "delicate."

Our first proof that mother and daughter were living together in the Toronto area was information from official school records. Dorothy had entered grade seven (Junior 4th) at Thornhill school in September 1921. We were mystified at first as to whether Thornhill was the name of the school or the name of the town where the school was located. There is a Thornhill street in Toronto, a block east of Brookside Avenue, but there was no school of that name in the district, and the archivist opined that the entry meant Thornhill Village in the North York Regional Board of Education.

We now know that Thornhill Public School, Union S.S. #1 Markham and Vaughan, was established in 1847. Even though the early building was burned down May 23, 1922, we still hoped to find early records to ascertain where mother attended school prior to 1921. The hope was unfulfilled. A search in 1999 confirmed all records had been destroyed.

By September 8, 1922, they were living at 11 Spadina Road, the home of Dr. Jabez Henry Elliott, where Grandma was employed as housekeeper. That same fall, Mother entered grade eight (Senior 4th) at Huron Street School in Toronto. Huron Street is a block or so east of Spadina Road. She wrote her high school entrance exams here in June of 1923. The doctor's wife, Mabel Amelia Tait, had died in July, leaving a young daughter Grace. Perhaps this is why Grandma was hired as housekeeper that summer. Knowing Grandma's compassion for youngsters, we surmise she cosetted the bereaved child, unwittingly forming a lifelong bond.

A noticeable thread throughout our research was confirmation of this continuing loyalty demonstrated by Grandma's Ontario and Quebec friends. In additon to her lifelong friendship with

Margaret MacDougall, her granddaughters well remember a loving relationship between Grandma and her former charge Grace when the two were visiting together. Then, too, a kindly old gentleman, Preston Lambert Tait, also came to visit us. A contemporary, he was the late Mrs. Elliott's brother, and the Taits had been born and raised in Bowmanville. Uncle Pres (as we were allowed to call him) lived in Vancouver when we knew him. Another close friend who came to see us all was Nora Kerslake, another Elliott relative, the daughter of Dr. Elliott's beloved sister, Mrs. C.J. Kerslake.

Grace and Mum seemed to act more like sisters who found pleasure in each other's company. We remember being excited in anticipation of Grace's visits to our home. An articulate story teller and very kind person, she would describe her well-travelled life with her husband, and the escapades of her children during several foreign U.N. postings.

Life had been very comfortable for Mum and Grandma while they lived with the doctor between 1921 and 1927. He was an important and prominent physician at St. Michaels Hospital and the Hospital for Sick Children, and a teacher at the University of Toronto where he had been educated.

Newspaper clippings described him as an international authority on tuberculosis and malaria, and the story of his career makes fascinating reading. A World War I medical officer, lecturer, writer, orator, historian and naturalist, he was president and officer of many medical organizations, and at his death in 1942, was eulogized as a significant contributor to Canada's medical profession.

The articles, obtained from the University of Toronto medical archives, drew a vivid portrait of this amazingly accomplished and busy man, who yet found time to appreciate his surroundings. One article claims that, "everywhere he went and chiefly in his beloved Muskoka, his senses were alive to the minutest details." One of his books was entitled *The Shrubs and Trees of Muskoka*. Now I know why Grandma always spoke of him with such respect.

The Teenager

Mother passed her exams, was issued an Ontario entrance certificate to a Collegiate in June, 1923, and began classes at Harbord in the fall. On all documents, her school's admission data described her mother as Mrs. Kathleen Scott, housekeeper and a Presbyterian.

On black-bordered velum stationery embossed with his Spadina road address is a note in the family archives, to wit:

June 15/ Dear Dorothy, Many happy returns of the day. Half of this is a birthday gift. Half is for getting your entrance recommendation. J.H. Elliott.

We have a picture taken about this time, of a plump teenager wearing glasses, with her hair loose around her face, sitting comfortably relaxed on a large rock. Smiling, Dorothy appears to be about age 14, wearing a dark coloured skirt and light coloured blouse. We have no idea where this picture might have been taken.

The first time Mother's name appeared in a street directory for either Ottawa or Toronto was in 1924 when Grandma was housekeeper for the doctor. Dorothy Scott, student, was categorized as a boarder.

A peek into the lives of two teenagers is eloquently provided in the following letters between Dorothy and her friend Grace. The warm relationship between the two girls is apparent, and under Kathleen's capable tutelage, flourished when they were brought together through Dr. Elliott's wise choice of his housekeeper, our resourceful Grandma.

After several years of close companionship the girls were parted when Grace began her studies at Ontario Ladies College in Whitby. The first of Dorothy's treasured letters is dated 1924.

Dear Dorothy!—

Just a note—we're in the midst of exams—
.....
I suppose you're having lots of fun—Marjory Marlow's tea is over? You're getting to be a gay young child.
(ahem! from my height and age of wisdom—child!) I think I'd better stop!
—Terribly dumb—but when you consider all that Caesar to be done by tomorrow afternoon and geometry! Oh boy!
—Much love, Grace.
(your mother doesn't deserve a letter all to herself because she hasn't written me. but I'll write on the back of this if you don't mind.)

Dear Mrs. Scott:
That box was just lovely! Thank you so much for going to all that trouble. We enjoyed everything so much—oh no, everything isn't eaten yet!

But thank you ever so—as I told Dorothy you don't deserve a real letter all to yourself, but of course I wanted to thank you— she'll know how busy I am—in spasms absolutely as you can probably tell from my scribbling!
Thanks again Mrs. Scott.
Lovingly,
Grace.

From Grace. Dated March 16, 1925.

Dear Dorothy:
What rotten luck! I'm so sorry—but never mind, you're getting better and you won't have to have another operation for a while—not on your appendix, anyway!
.....
Hope you can sit up soon!
Much love,
Grace.

From Grace. Dated March 24, 1925.

Dear Dorothy,
Here we are again! Just been practising for the senior stunt—a
little bit of a scene out of Dickens where a boy Harry Walmers
and I—Norah somebody run away.

Exams start Thursday and oh boy, if you could only see the
plan we have for decorating the gym—and all these practices.
More darn fun! We got our paper today—we ordered 8 dozen
rolls of apple green crepe—and the shade we got is the most bil-
ious yellow you could imagine—so we have to send for more—
Pat phoned her father and he's getting it from a wholesale
house—otherwise we'd have a choice bill! for we're getting six
dozen white too!

Latin Prose for an hour now—I've bummed the last half hour
and didn't do it—as usual. Lily's going to get mad at me some-
day maybe.

This is the other side of our room. My dresser—a wicker chair
with Harry's picture over it—it's great. Table with the vic. a
lamp a pile of books and a few magazines. My bed with much
soot blowing in on the end of it through the storm window—an
awful nuisance and our rugs! Don't forget them. Our room is
20' long by 9' across with two tall windows at the right of this
picture.

You shall have to admire this picture for I'm doing it in Latin
and Sunny and Aileen think its "cute" even if the pictures are
crooked and everything out of proportion.

Only nine days more! I've been trying to decide whether or not
to ask Nina home for a few days, but—which suddenly occurs
to me—your mother will be busy enough without someone
extra. And anyway probably her father won't let her. She's six-
teen and her father is eighty four—imagine! And he's awfully set
in his ways—His home is in Michigan.

I really must pay attention to what Lily's putting on the
board—she's been giving me several glances—

I'll mail this on the way to the printers. We're having pro-
grammes for Saturday evening.
Much love to you,
Grace.

The following, undated letter, from Dorothy, was not in an envelope. The underlining of certain words was by Dorothy. I found
it odd that Mother had in her possession a letter she had written
to her friend.

Ma Cherie Gracia,

I am up! and dressed and walking around. I have a choice stoop
but I think that it will wear away soon. Outside is grey and dull.
A cold biting wind blows the rain in true March style. I am in
the sitting room at the square card table. A fire is rustling and
crackling in the fire place and Billy is near me. Oh how cosy it
all looks. Poor, poor Nina. I felt like crying myself when I read
about her. Imagine not having either father or mother. The
weather seem so cold and dreary I'm sure if anything happened
to me in such weather I should feel so alone and unloved even
nature would seems to have turned her back cold and unfeeling.
Can you understand what I <u>am trying</u> to tell you? I feel queer
today. Again, perhaps it is the weather.

Today was a red letter day for me. I hear that somebody is
going to be eighteen soon. Well well, well. Bless my whiskers
<u>this</u> child will be <u>sixteen</u> soon. I am afraid to grow up. I, like
Peter Pan want forever to be young! Perhaps I will stay young
that is my feeling well but it seems that old people who feel
young are thought to be crazy. Cruel, unkind, wouldn't say cut-
ting things about them. Billy has never seen an open fire before
and is intensely interested by the flames. He is singing to them.
How do you like my classy stationery. Flossy, huh? There were
two terrifically funny jokes in the Tely last night. I'll see if I can
find them. If I do, I'll send them to you. I found them. Please
find enclosed etc. etc.

72

*Marge Elliott has been looking for a letter for a long time.
She's making dire threats if she doesn't see you or get a letter. I'm
embroidering (?) towels for our M.B. bazaar. They are quite
pretty. Oh, dear! I do want to see that school so badly. Feeling
bad about leaving it are you not? I would. You set me nearly
crazy describing that room and the water at Ports. How could
you be so mean? when I have to go three months yet and over
nine more exams?*

*I can still feel the magic touch of the water 'gainst my skin in
the night of the dark of the moon. Whitings orchestra murmur-
ing Marcheta soft swishing of wavelet on Standishs beach. A
purring launch chanting voices and tinkling uke drifting home-
wards via the Indian River. Deep soft shadows pale yellow lights
and two white sprites on a wharf of pale grey. Looks like velvet
feels like tacks. Ouch muttered cusses and the spell is broken.
Come girls you've been in long enough. Aw just one more. No
come in. Rustling of raincoats delicious shivers and bed.*

Love, Dorothy.

Mother had told us her appendix had been removed. Perhaps
this is what she is describing when she comments on the "choice
stoop," a familiar pose when recovering from abdominal sur-
gery. Port Carling, Muskoka, is the location when she speaks of
"Ports."

At first we were confused by her reference to "nine or more
exams." Her school records showed that the first time so many
exams were taken was in June 1926. However, there is now no
doubt her appendix operation occurred in 1925. We don't know
how many school days she missed as a result, but she was ill
again in the winter term of 1926 missing eight full days and two
half days of school, which were mentioned on her June report
card. Her reference to "being 16 soon" confirms the age she
gave to the Ontario Registrar in 1967.

Mother and Dad attended a mutual friend's house party
towards the end of 1926. Dad told his mother the next night he

had met the girl he intended to marry. A cropped picture of Dorothy, apparently ready to set out for a ride on her bicycle, is quite charming. The words on the back of the picture read as follows: "Taken down at Marge's in Blackstock last summer. Aren't my glasses fetching? I know you will like this picture of me on account of them. D." Blackstock was a small town north of Bowmanville near Lake Scugog. We believe Mum sent this picture to Dad in Hamilton, where he had been posted by his company, soon after their meeting at Lillian's. He carried the snapshot for many years, after cutting it to size to fit in his wallet.

Grandma heard in January of 1927 that Dorothy had become engaged. Letters were exchanged between Dad and Mum while he was vacationing with his sister in Muskoka.

On January 30, 1927, Father wrote, "I thought you were going to let me tell your mother of our plans... I certainly don't believe in long engagements... What does your mother say about your marrying so young? Now that your mother knows we are to be married some fine day...."

Dorothy wrote her Middle School examinations wearing her diamond engagement ring. The results of her exams were issued in June of 1927. She did poorly.

Aunt Sarah Adams had reached her 78th birthday in February 1927 and had made a new will in March, naming Bessie Louise Cook as her sole legatee, noting that Bessie had lived with her for "ten years and more."

Grandma's happy employment with the doctor ended the same year, 1927, but we are not sure why. Perhaps there were objections to this proposed marriage by both Aunt Sarah and Dr. Elliott.

Mother was very young when the news of her engagement was presented, and there was great disparity in the ages of the couple. Dad was a very handsome man about town, and may have been perceived in an unflattering light by the doctor. The doctor and Grandma could have disagreed about the need for haste in planning young Dorothy's future.

Grandma may have voiced her view that marriage seemed the ultimate security for her daughter—a security Katie would never know. The facts surrounding Dorothy's birth may have been revealed in the ensuing discussion, and the doctor, affronted by the unpleasant news, may have asked Grandma to leave his employ.

Or perhaps a full-time housekeeper was simply no longer essential while Dr. Elliott travelled extensively. The timing simply might have been propitious. His daughter was grown, had finished her schooling, and may have been ready to take over the reins of the household.

However, Grandma told my brother that our other grandmother also tried to end the relationship between Mother and Dad. In a face-to-face confrontation with Kathleen, "she felt that Dorothy and her background were not good enough for her son." A revealing comment, which lends credence to our suspicion of a confrontation between Grandma and her employer.

My conviction is that Kathleen always supported the plans for Dad and Mum to marry, and I know that Dad always treated Grandma with great respect. He had opined that she would "raise a howl," and she did not. I also think Kathleen was very deeply concerned about Dorothy's security and made it a primary goal, allying herself with the affianced couple in their plans for the future, against all odds. I also think that something in Dad's character and/or demeanour struck a chord of memory with Kathleen—a memory of people known in Scotland as a child. Admiring his strength of purpose, perhaps, and his ability to overcome obstacles, she recognized a safe haven for her daughter.

Marriage

My parents were married June 30th, 1928 in Toronto. The newspaper description read, in part:

*The bride, who was given away by Mr. George Langley,
looked charming in a gown of white georgette and silver lace,
with large white maline hat, velvet trimmed, and carried a shower bouquet of Butterfly roses and baby's breath. The bridesmaid
was Miss Grace Elliott, in a frock of beige georgette, with hat to
match, and bouquet of mauve sweet peas. The groom was
attended by Mr. Nelson Teeple, and during the signing of the
register Miss Ruth Robertson, sister of the groom, sang "For
You Alone." After a brief honeymoon the happy couple will
reside in Toronto at the Victoria Park Apartments.*

The song that Ruth sang for her brother and his new bride
gives us a clue about their very romantic relationship. The music
was composed by Henry E. Geehli, with lyrics by P.J. O'Reilly:

*Take thou this rose, this little tender rose
The rarest flower in all God's garden.*

*And let be, while yet its crimson grows
An emblem of the love, I proudly, proudly bear.*

*Take thou this heart, the heart that loves thee well
And let it flame before thy shrine
My own.
Take thou my heart, for, oh, your dear eyes tell
God fashioned it for you.
For you alone.*

A modest family supper reception was held afterwards at a
restaurant called The Diet Kitchen on Bloor Street. One of the
guests was George Langley. Since he gave the bride away, there
must have been a connection with Dorothy and Kathleen. What
was the connection? His name is not familiar to any of the
grandchildren, nor did we find a link when we researched his
family history. Another small puzzle to solve when time allows.

When I was redrafting my manuscript I realized this marriage must have had enormous importance for Grandma. The destitute Scottish orphan had successfully overcome many obstacles to raise her daughter, doggedly determined to protect her from economic deprivation and social rejection. Proudly, she was able to see her beloved child safely married to a fine young man, her future assured. I would guess it made tiny Katie extremely happy!

Mother had told us that attendance at Presbyterian Sunday school and church had been a childhood requirement. She often expressed distaste for restrictions she felt the church had placed upon her, and the amount of time she had had to spend in church activities. Perhaps this explains why the marriage took place in an Anglican Church, even though Dad's family followed the Christian Science church precepts. She never attended church when we knew her, except for special ceremonies such as marriages and baptisms. She did not prevent her children from going to Sunday School, but I regret that I do not recall her ever encouraging our attendance.

Grandma wrote her maiden name as Catherine Scott on the 1928 Ontario marriage form and the father of bride was listed as "not known." We were initially puzzled by what seemed to be a spelling error in Grandma's name. Much later, closer examination made us realize that this official registration document was our first real clue as to Grandma's identity, and further research, of course, confirmed it. Dorothy's address was a boarding house on Sherbourne Street but Grandma's address that summer is still unconfirmed.

It would seem Dad's notes had been correct, in that Grandma's employment with Dr. Elliott ended in 1927, sometime after the engagement was announced. This could explain why Dorothy worked in an office for a few months before her marriage. How difficult was it for Kathleen to find work after the years at Elliott's? We know she began working at the CPR in June of 1929, but what did she do in the interim?

The young couple had no money for a honeymoon, and instead spent the time at Toronto Beach. After six weeks of marriage Dad began work as assistant travelling auditor, and was sent on a three month western tour of offices. He was home for Christmas, and later audited branches in Ontario awaiting the birth of their first child.

A Canadian Pacific Railway Company document dated April 1934 attests to Grandma's floor clerk service from June 10, 1929, to December 1, 1932, and is in the family archives. Two months before she started work at the Royal York Hotel her first grandchild was born at St. Michael's hospital, and she was able to help her daughter through the first months after the birth.

Dad began auditing at the Montreal branch of his company in the fall of 1929, and returned the next March, coming home every second week to visit his wife and child. Dorothy had to cope alone. Fortunately, Kathleen was nearby. Posted back to the Toronto office for a few weeks in the spring of 1930, Dad was then transferred permanently to Montreal. The family lived first at a hotel, then moved to a small apartment on Queen Mary Road.

In Ottawa, Aunt Sarah Adams died after a long illness in the winter of 1930. She was buried near her sister Annie in Auld Kirk Cemetery, Almonte. The obituary included the names of her daughter, Mrs. R.L. Hornidge of Toronto, and her granddaughter, Bessie Louise Cook of Ottawa. This seemed strange, as Sarah didn't have any children. She married William when she was 47, too old to start a family, although she listed her age as 40. A spinster, Sarah had worked in a factory for years, then started a "Fancy Store" with her sister, always living in her parents' Almonte home.

Sarah's will, written in March of 1927, was probated in early January of 1931. There was no reference to Kathleen Scott, Ida Adams, or Mrs. R.L. Hornidge. Bessie Louise Cook is the only legatee. The section requesting information concerning the relationship of the deceased to the legatee on the court document is left blank. This indicates to me that Sarah and Bessie were not blood kin.

To our surprise, Bessie's address quoted in the will was the same as the 1914 address for Sarah's sister and her nieces Margaret and Evelyn Sara. But who was Mrs. R.L. Hornidge? We know her husband, Robert Leonard, was born in Ottawa in 1888, and grew up a few blocks away from the Adams family. He moved to Toronto, where we found him listed as a boarder on Brookside Avenue in 1929.

Was there any connection at all between the Hornidge name and our Kathleen? The families were neighbours. Did she know them more intimately when she lived with the Adams? More intensive research will be required to solve this aspect of the mystery. We could not seem to locate Mrs. Hornidge's maiden name with sources available to us. However, having examined the Ontario marriage records up to and including 1921, we estimate that the marriage took place after 1921 and before the December 1930 obituary reference to Mrs. Hornidge. Unfortunately, the 1933 obituary for Robert Leonard's mother doesn't help either, as only her surviving issue were named.

The casual way unrelated people were designated as relatives in Sarah's life made me wonder if Kathleen could have been treated in a similar manner. When Grandma spoke to me of Aunt Sarah, perhaps she meant more than a graciousness of speech. It is possible Kathleen was absorbed into Sarah's small group, and that when she used the word "Aunt," it meant a close relationship.

When I used the word "casual" in the above paragraph to describe Sarah Adams' acceptance of relatives, I'm thinking of it in the sense of not being formally entered into records. The deaths of her five sisters, and her adopted daughter, Florence, makes me wonder if her acceptance of various young people into her home was a direct result of her reaction to these losses. I visualize a fiercely loyal and protective Sarah. Her habit of changing dates of birth in census and death records follows a pattern, to me, of trying to fit events to protect the reputation of those people she cared about. I have noticed this pattern of age changes throughout my research on Sarah, Kathleen, and Dorothy. It seems to have been convenient for all of them. Sarah began to do it in the first instance at the time of her marriage, and then for census purposes. Kathleen and Dorothy used the device as well. To protect themselves? From what?

Grandma had told me, with some bitterness, that "they took my money." Who or what was she referring to? Was it perhaps the family who were supposed to pay her a small salary during her childhood indenture at the farm? Or was she referring to people connected with Aunt Sarah?

We may never be able to fully establish Kathleen or Dorothy's complete early history as so many records have been destroyed. The inconsistencies encountered in trying to confirm their stories, though, cast a benevolent doubt on what we were told as children. Even so, we hope the portrayal of Grandma's life will lead to an understanding of her challenges and how they were met.

In 1931, mail for Grandma was "care of" Mrs. Margaret MacDougall, 96 Campbell Avenue, Toronto (yes, the same friend on Mark Street where Grandma had been boarding in 1912). Margaret MacDougall lived at this address from 1925 to 1935 and moved to St. Clair Avenue in 1937, and from 1938 until at least 1941 was listed at Nairn Avenue. Where she lived in the missing years 1917 to 1924 is still a mystery.

Obviously, Grandma and Margaret had remained friends all those years and I wonder if they shared experiences during World War I, too. Perhaps they worked together in one of the Toronto munitions plants, since Margaret's husband had joined the Canadian Expeditionary Force in 1917, had been invalided home and Margaret was then required to earn her living.

Dad and Mum subletted a Queen Mary Road apartment and moved to larger digs at Earnscliffe Avenue in the spring of 1931, awaiting the birth of Kathleen's second granddaughter, who was born in May. Dad would have made sure he knew where to contact Grandma to advise her on the progress of her daughter's second pregnancy. But why didn't Kathleen have a stable place to live, and why was her mail being directed to her friend in 1931?

The mystery is further complicated by an unfortunate incident. One day my brother and I were examining the contents of a large brown suitcase which held the family archives. While sorting out batches of old letters, wills, pictures and empty envelopes, we found a press clipping, picturing the marriage of a Mrs. Kathleen Scott, who seemed to be a person in her 40's. Since it appeared to be someone we did not know, with coincidentally the same name as our grandma, we threw it out!

The blurred newspaper photograph could have been of our grandma, but we had not yet seen any pictures of her as a young woman. We learned a very hard lesson. Even though it might not be readily apparent to the sorters, someone had a logical reason for keeping the clipping. How many times since have we castigated ourselves for doing this awful thing! We don't even remember the man's name, except that it was lengthy. It could very well have been our grandma's wedding picture, taken around 1929 or 1930.

But who was the groom? Thinking it could possibly be people we had already encountered, we wondered about Robert Leonard Hornidge, considering the lengthiness of his name. He had lived near the Adams family in Ottawa and then went to live in west central Toronto. He was also the same age as Grandma. Robert could have resumed a friendship with Kathleen while she worked at the Royal York Hotel because he might have stayed there on his travels as a salesman for his company. His family had Toronto contacts from his father's training as a policeman in that city. Grandma had used the name Robert for her father; had chosen the name of Robert's sister Kathleen; and had named her daughter Dorothy, the name of Robert's little sister who died in Ottawa in 1886, the year of grandma's birth.

All true, but no positive link had been established. We were only guessing. To our amazement, in the fall of 1998, we were fortunate enough to make contact with a Hornidge granddaughter, and discovered that Robert had married Aunt Sarah's niece, Margaret Hamilton.

Margaret's granddaughter told me that the Hamilton girls lived with their Aunt Sarah after the death of their mother. She also told me that all the girls who lived with Sarah called her "Aunt" and each other, "cousin." The backgrounds of Sarah's other youngsters were unknown to the Hornidge descendants, and they were astonished at my revelation that Grandma was a Home Child.

Whispers in the Hornidge family about Aunt Sarah's young children, which had suggested possible illegitimacy, were remembered. They had always been curious about these particular secrets. Now, however, they have written to Quarriers hoping to establish when and where all the other girls were born, including Bessie Louise Cook, who was Margaret Hamilton Hornidge's best friend.

Still unresolved are the reasons our own Grandma came to choose the names used in her legend. Perhaps the answer is as simple as the fact she used names she had heard.

V

Grandchildren

One of the many interesting aspects of our research was trying to reconstruct Grandma's life after the family was transferred to Montreal and before her permanent move to the Lakeshore. To this end we gathered together the family photographs and tried to put them in chronological order. As you can imagine there were some wonderful, revelatory discussions while we figured it all out!

We couldn't find any taken at our Montreal apartments, but this may have meant we simply didn't own a camera until later. Starting in 1932, several pictures were taken the in the garden of our first Lakeshore house. One is of Kathleen's year-old granddaughter in diapers, held up by her Grandma as the child reaches for her lapel brooch. Grandma noticed that this grandchild had developed rickets, caused by a vitamin D deficiency, and told the young parents how to help the child. This story was recalled during our discussions.

Another picture, this time of the eldest grandchild, clasped in her mother's right arm as she stoops to hug her, shows a face which is an exact replica of the Quarriers child who came to Canada at age 10. The resemblance is remarkable, and reassured us when it seemed too incredible that we had been able to establish her identity!

As Dad wrote in his memoirs, Grandma came in April 1934 to help him move to a larger house at the western end of the village, while Mum was still in hospital with Kathleen's first grand-

son.   One   of Grandma's cherished pictures, of a skinny mite of a child stand- ing in front of this newer house, has the following message on the back: "Hello, Grandma, will this do? Thank you for the card. This is my answer." The message was in response to a 1934 birthday card. Then, during a lull in her domestic duties, a slender Kathleen was photographed taking her grandson for a walk in his new carriage. My sister remembers when the new carriage arrived, as well as how modern it looked in comparison with her enormous old wicker one. Since Grandma was wearing a short-sleeved cot- ton dress, we concluded the picture was taken in the summer of 1934.

After only one year in the western part of the village, the fam- ily moved again, this time to a house in the centre of town and closer to the lake, where they remained for 13 years. Grandma was photographed on the verandah, and while only their heads appear, the child with her looks to be about age four, which would mean it was 1935. Chatting about something they see in the foreground, the two faces are serene.

Another photo shows Kathleen sitting in a deck chair, with her two grand-daughters seated on the foot rest in front of her. The faces of Kathleen and her oldest grandchild are extraordinarily similar in expression and features. It is summer, and the youngsters appear to be about ages four and six, and since one child has exactly the same hairdo as in the paragraph above, this would also be in 1935. My sister remembers her  Grandma intervening during a beating by her mother, with the words "Dorothy! She's only six!" This would further confirm Kathleen's regular visits with the family through the 1930's, as well as her distaste for excessive discipline of young children. Grandma came to visit again in the summer of 1937 to help

 prior to the birth of Dorothy's fourth child, who was born in September at the same Lachine hospital where his older brother had been born.

In the next photograph, an eight-year-old granddaughter looks very pleased to be with her Grandma, whose left arm is clasped tightly around her in what looks to be a gesture of comfort. Standing in front of our stone wall and garden, Kathleen is wearing a house dress and looks very weary. The care of three young children, a son-in-law, and a pregnant daughter on your vacation could lead to a state of weariness!

Always ready, willing and able to help the family in any emergency, perhaps this was a detriment to Kathleen's employment record. If she was not able to schedule time away from her employment each time Dorothy was about to give birth, she may have had to change her employment. This could, in part, explain the long list of her addresses, and types of employment in those years. Of course, it was during the Depression, and she may have had to pick up whatever job she could, when work was available. And there may have been long stretches of time between jobs, leaving her free to attend to her daughter.

Her staff record at the Royal York Hotel indicated her employment at CPR ended December 1st, 1932 though Kathleen still used the CPR connection when giving address and employment to Might's Directories after 1934, using, as well, the reference, "widow of Norman." It is possible these two bits of information were fanciful details, not absolute fact, since we have not yet found confirmation Grandma was ever married. And whether or not she worked for CPR after April of 1934 remains

to be seen. CPR has informed me that staff records are no longer open to genealogists and another source of information has not been found.

We know that Grandma visited again in the spring of 1938, prior to moving here permanently, as we have a picture taken with our neighbour Grandpa Edwards holding her infant grandson while his four year old brother stands close to his grandma's side. Kathleen is wearing very plain dark clothing, with a somber expression on her face.

This particular photograph disturbed me, and I wasn't sure why. Perhaps the unusual lack of joy on the faces, except for the baby, and the dark clothing were expressing unexplained unhappiness in the family.

My supposition turned out to be true.

Another War

The Second World War began in September of 1939, but another war was already being waged within the family. These years would affect their lives substantially—and forever. Kathleen's integral role in the rearing of the children would expand and her presence would become very important in their lives as events that seemed unrelated at the time, combined to alter their personal relationships.

One of the purposes of this part of Kathleen's story was to try and understand what these events were, the role of the adults, and the effect on the children. From memories of the grandchildren, factual events, and some speculation, we tried to piece together what really happened.

Dorothy later told her eldest daughter in a moment of confidence that she had had her fifth child aborted. We are not sure which year the event occurred, but 1938 seems likely. We don't know if the decision to abort the child had been made over her objections, or whether husband and wife were in agreement. What we do know, however, is that a lifelong chemical dependency began when she was prescribed phenobarbitol to help her sleep when she was 30. My brother recalls his mother's penchant for sherry as early as 1941. Something of magnitude must have occurred to make such a lasting impression on the four-year-old child.

Kathleen's history as an abused child—surviving in a society that considered her life contemptuous, being an unwed mother who nevertheless carried her child to term in spite of prevailing attitudes, working extremely hard all her life to help her child, supporting her child's decision to marry young in the face of many odds, aiding her daughter at the birth of each grandchild, and travelling from Toronto to be at her side—makes me believe that Kathleen valued every grandchild's life, and would have done anything to help with the fifth child. Grandma's anger must have been enormous, and she would have expressed her strong disapproval of abortion to her daughter.

I remember how harshly Grandma verbally chastised her grandchildren when our actions offended her view of acceptable conduct. A terrible confrontation must have occurred. I do not know what was said, but Dorothy's irascibility towards her mother was very noticeable thereafter. The children first noticed signs of withdrawal when Dorothy stayed in bed for weeks, probably devasted by the aftermath of the whole painful abortion episode, as well as her mother's verbal assault. As her reliance on alcohol and prescription drugs increased through the years, "don't upset your mother" became a frequent instruction to the children.

An inability to confront the problem or its underlying cause exacerbated its impact on the family. The children received less and less emotional support and were drawn into a world of denial. As mother's stability gradually decreased, an indulgent husband's primary concern became the alleviation of his beloved's pain. The children were left to solve their own problems, and often wistfully turned to their Grandma. Kathleen once more tried to help, comforting her grandchildren when she could, always making herself available to them. But it would not be surprising if she did not fully understand the causes or the severity of her daughter's problem.

> *I have done nothing but in care of thee,*
> *Of thee my dear one, thee my daughter, who*
> *Art ignorant of what thou art, naught knowing*
> *Of whence I am....*
>
> —The Tempest

How much did Grandma know about her family, and how much did she tell her daughter? Were her oblique references to "a long line of Stuarts" an implication that she knew more about her history, felt shame she had been rejected, and kept the details secret? Societal attitudes at the time would also have negated any wish to be more forthcoming about her experiences as a Home Child. In any case, what Dorothy believed and how she reacted to this belief played an integral role in future family relationships.

The Village

Feeling too confined in my apartment one day, I tucked my manuscript under my arm and went for a long, nostalgic walk. I saw the verandahs where we had played rainy-day Monopoly, and the windows where we had lodged our Toddy tin telephones. Happily, the changes to our favourite old street were mostly cosmetic, since only one house had been demolished. The fields behind our house, once perfect for hide-and-seek and run-sheep-run, had been developed for suburban housing.

Heading to the foot of the street I realized that our swimming bay of the 1940's was gone. A new breakwater and landfill had turned it into a grassy, treed park, furnished with several benches and picnic tables—a breezy, pleasant spot to relax on a hot summer afternoon and muse about another era. Refreshed, I sat down, opened my binder and began to write.

We had moved to our first Lakeshore house—in Pointe-Claire—in 1932. A small French-colonial with 18-inch thick stone walls, it was centred on a beautifully treed lot. This stone house now sits at the southern edge of the property close to a newer building, but its solid yet graceful beauty still impresses the viewer. The deeply recessed doorway is balanced by a floor-to-ceiling glass door on each side. The house is enhanced by dormer windows and a sharply sloping roof. As there is just enough living space for a family of four, its original owners had added a small ground-floor music room which still nestles against the main house. Awaking on his first Lakeshore morning, to the beautiful perfume of lilacs drifting through his bedroom window Dad called it his dream house, and I can understand why.

Even though I was very young I can still remember living in that house. I vividly recall the spring day my sister grabbed the neck of my snowsuit and pulled me to safety from the deep water ditch behind the house. Another time, having been bitten on the face by the neighbour's cranky little black dog, Dr. Parke prescribed half an orange, plus a peppermint he took from his pocket. It was a big deal having a doctor call at the house—this was indeed an event for me to remember!

As the family increased, we moved to our second house at the west end of the village. It was a big, bleak, unfriendly house and we stayed there only a year. Then we settled on our favourite street in the centre of the village where we stayed for over 13 years.

When we first lived in the village there was no post office, library or bus service. The town was surrounded by farms. Few roads were paved and people travelled by horses and wagons. Protestant and Catholic churches tried to keep their congregations separated, usually without success. Kindred spirits found each other whichever language or religion they professed. Ice boxes were the norm in kitchens. Delivered daily, the ice blocks had been cut from the lake in the winter, and stored in straw at the village ice house. In the summer, delivery men would occasionally chip off delicious slivers for thirsty children.

Local farmers sold produce door to door in season, although some families grew their own. Vegetables and fruit were first rate, bread and milk, less so. The local bakery and dairy delivered year round, but the bread was coarse, hardy, and molasses-brown. Healthful, probably, but we yearned for the more delicate, white bread sandwiches. Watered prior to delivery, the milk had a pale blue cast, though there was still a layer of cream at the top, which froze and protruded above the bottletop in winter. A quick scraping tasted delicious to the lucky child retrieving the milk from the doorstep.

Small purchases of meat could be made at the village butcher shop. To avoid disappointment in cut or freshness, housewives made a point of shopping in person, though even then the butcher's thumb on the scale added a few more cents per pound. Larger meat purchases were phoned in to Eaton's or Pesner's in downtown Montreal. Staples were also ordered through Eaton's, though occasionally when mothers needed a break they would make the trek downtown by bus and return home tired but content late in the afternoon.

Without cars, fathers travelled to their Montreal offices by train and were deposited a mere half hour later at Bonaventure or Windsor stations. Money was scarce, clothing purchases few, and kind out-of-town friends shipped large cartons of cast-offs which we picked up at the CN train station.

Summers were spent playing games with neighbourhood children. Hop scotch, run-sheep-run, hide and seek, and tag were games for the littlest angels; baseball, football, tennis, sailing, cards and board games were played by the older children. Games were interrupted when all hands were needed in hot summer kitchens to help mothers prepare the ingredients for pickled vegetables, preserved fruits, and jugged marmalade. A forbidden treat, nevertheless sampled from the chip wagon when a nickel was available, was a pungent bag of french fries. Piping hot, salted, and splashed with vinegar, they were ambrosia to a young palate.

In the fall and spring we ate our lunches quickly and sped back to school to play baseball until the bell rang for classes. We returned much more slowly on very cold winter days chewing dried prunes to keep our cheeks from freezing. Winter weekends were spent at the golf course, skiing and tobogganing, led by our vigorous father, or skating on Lake St. Louis after Dad had tested and plowed the ice. We built huge snow forts whenever possible for the inevitable neighbourhood snowball wars.

Dances were held before the war at the Maples Inn and Edgewater Hotel and mothers would happily create colourful inexpensive ball gowns, watched by their young daughters who wondered what all the fuss was about. Golf and curling were available for families with funds, while the Yacht Club became the less expensive summer focus for others. Besides sailing activities planned by the men, social gatherings were organized by "lady associates," the wives and daughters of the members, who, much later, were finally granted full membership to the club. There were sailing races, shared boat chores, picnics aboard *Curlew*, and chilly swims after a sail. There were also adventures aboard *Thalia Ann* when the skipper, aided by his youthful exhuberant crew, coped with serious, and sometimes hilarious emergencies.

We attended Sunday school, sang in the church choir, and belonged to both Anglican and United Church Young People's associations. Carefully chaperoned, we danced in school gyms, always ending the evening with Artie Shaw's "Stardust." We competed in school field-day events, prepared food baskets for the poor at Christmas, and helped with special wartime projects. We gambled at the yearly tombolas while loud speakers blared Doris Day's "Sentimental Journey," cheered the local team at baseball games, and laughed till we were weak at dreadful band concerts in Laroque Park.

We heard honourable and dishonourable visitors make windy political speeches, watched solemn children in white suits and dresses march in the St. Jean Baptiste parade, and stood in respectful silence by the side of the road whenever a funeral procession passed. We secretively overheard adult conversations which we rarely understood, gulped summer refreshments with other kids under the catalpa tree, gossiped with elderly neighbours over dainty cups of weak tea, giggled at the silly yarns of visitors, and were curious about the opposite sex.

This, then, was the backdrop for the evolution of one Lakeshore family.

Warp and Weft

Grandma lived with us when she first moved to the Lakeshore. Dad helped her get a new set of teeth prior to starting a housekeeping job at a house further up our street. It was while living in that house Grandma acquired her purebred Cairn Terrier she called MacDuff (Duffy). Duffy and Grandma were inseparable for many years. His stiff-textured coat and moist, beady eyes, as well as his fondness for attention and petting are well remembered by all of us.

In our search for validation of the exact year Grandma settled in the province, we were awaiting information from Statistics Canada on whether or not Kathleen registered under the National Resources Mobilization Act of 1940. On July 14, 1997, StatsCan wrote to say no information has been found on either Catherine or Kathleen Scott either as an Ontario or Quebec resident. There could be two explanations for this. One, the bureaucrats in this province were reluctant to comply with the registration requirement, as part of their distaste for the law's perceived connection to conscription. The other reason could be Kathleen's reluctance to answer some of the questions posed in the registration form. Even though the law as written carried severe penalties for non-compliance, avoiding the commitment to register, I understand, was not that difficult.

It is suggested in the Heritage Renfrew literature that many Home Children did not even apply for social security or pension benefits later on, because they did not know they could. Without documents, perhaps application would have seemed impossible.

My brother remembers visiting his Grandma Scott at her home up the street when he was a little tyke of 4. It was not too far a walk for a toddler. The girls remember that they were required to assume responsibility, at a very early age, for cooking their father's breakfast, doing the housecleaning and laundry on Saturdays as well as the nightly dishwashing after Kathleen left

93

us. Mother continued with the cooking and sewing, becoming an excellent baker and seamstress.

One day I was harshly beaten with a hairbrush by my mother during the school lunch break. Catching me swearing at my sister and including the word "bastard," Mother took aggressive action. I find this significant to Dorothy's story, and illustrative of her distaste for the word.

My sister was also a recipient of mother's rage and was beaten with a piece of orange crate in front of the neighbourhood children. The cause is forgotten, but not the dismay and humiliation. In any case, Kathleen was not present to intervene for her grandchildren on these occasions. Several times the girls received large lumps of coal in lieu of candy in their Christmas stockings, but we were too ashamed to tell Grandma. She never knew.

On another occasion Mother ruled that my sister was no longer allowed to read during the week. She could do so on weekends, but only after her homework was completed and she had received permission from mother. As a result, my sister remembers memorizing the titles of all the books in the family bookcase, but had never read their contents. I had not known about this vicious punishment of a child who led her class in elementary school. While adjusting to her mother's dictum, her marks began to drop and she was never able to fully restore her previous achievement at the top of her class. During our discussions this year my sister and I tried to guess the reasons for Dorothy's incredible action, but as yet do not have an answer.

I clearly remember reading all of the books. Two of them, *The Head of the House of Coombe* and *Robin*, by Frances Hodgson Burnett, were companion novels concerning a naive young woman, pregnant after an intimate relationship with a soldier on leave from duty in France, who was later rescued by the soldier's wealthy father. At the time, the books meant nothing more to me than good stories carefully preserved for years in mother's library. Later, knowing more of Dorothy's history, I wondered if she was still struggling for answers to her own mother's circumstances and found comfort in the romantic portrayal. Susan M.

94

Trotsky, a Burnett scholar, explains in *Contemporary Authors* that, "In these and similar works, a sort of rags-to-riches achievement is realized wherein a simple, good hearted heroine gains understanding from more socially prominent figures."

However, I recently managed to obtain copies of the books and in the rereading discovered to my amazement that they were, in essence, a lengthy portrait of the extreme loneliness of an intelligent female child, denied normal childhood contacts and experiences. I believe Mother empathized with the child, recognizing in the heroine a similar adult desire for continued protection from life's vicissitudes.

I begin to see a relationship between Dorothy's reluctance to describe her early youth to her children and her preferred remembrance of her teenage years living with her mother in the wide Elliott family circle. We believe her early childhood years, when she and her beloved mother experienced prolonged separations, may have been too painful to recall.

Early in the war years, Mother no longer had Grandma's household assistance, nor that of a series of maids who had helped out over the years. Was she overwhelmed by her role as a housewife and mother of four young children? Or was her rage a demonstration of her distress over her mother's revelations? Both are likely, since we know that up to this time her relationship with her mother had been extremely loving.

It would have been a profound shock for Dorothy to learn about Katie's childhood status and her own birth during the confrontation with her mother. In the more rigid social norms of the times, she could have feared becoming a pariah in her small town should the story be known. And the conflict could have tormented her. Early ignorance of her mother's story is supported by the October 1934 marriage entry in the family Bible. Norman Scott and Kathleen Harvey are cited as Dorothy's parents.

I suspect that when subsequent name changes were made in Dad's notes, he overlooked the possible existence of a legal Ontario registration document, certifying Grandma's real maiden name was Catherine Scott, and the father of the bride was "unknown." Dad's files contained only the brief church certificate, and as I found out, the official Church register was also devoid of family details. The witnesses signed what was essentially a blank page except for the names of the bride and groom. When Dad later prepared his notes for the family history he realized he had a problem and confused the issue further with crossed out name entries. He too, was conflicted, between loyalty to his wife and the true story.

My sister and I believe the emotionally vulnerable young woman was very troubled by the disclosures and her anger towards her mother. The burden may have been too great for her fragile psyche, and unable to accept or forgive, her chemical dependency deepened. The children had no knowledge of the cause of their mother's unhappiness, were drawn into a pattern of accepting guilt for innocent actions, and were greatly affected by the unhealthy family dynamic that developed.

We hoped that ferretting out the full story, even at this late date, would at least break the circle of silence, allowing a healing process to begin. In fact, we think it already has. Affirming they were not at fault for their Mother's problem was very important to her children, and greatly lessened the emotional burden they had assumed on behalf of their parents.

We also realized how Agnes Scott's decisions in 1892, like pebbles tossed in a pond, caused ripples that eventually affected four generations.

The Inner Child

Some pencilled scribblings in Mother's handwriting were found amongst old family pictures in the summer of 1998. Considering Dad's dated accompanying article, and the fact that they were all on pages of the same brownish-coloured paper, we surmise they were written in the late nineteen thirties.

The themes and certain sentences could suggest an inner battle which Dorothy had tried to express fictionally. Saved for nearly fifty years, we recognize how much these bits and pieces of stories meant to her. Untitled, they begin as follows:

Ruth had been a shy moody child given to wild outbursts that adults had called temper.

A small child crisply pinafored, sat sedately rocking her doll. She got up from her chair and moved slowly out of the room. With tears in her eyes her mother gazed after her, pain, love and incomprehension written on her face.

What a strange child for herself and her husband to have borne—they were both of middle build, inclined to plumpness and in their youth cheerful, fond of good company and a (blank).

But since this changeling had come to them how different they were. As a tiny infant she had been given to sudden violent outbursts of crying—in spite of all attentions, soothing remedies, she continued to scream, while her desparate young mother held her close in terror stricken love. As she grew older, she grew no better.

In spite of doctors advices and reassurances as to her bodily and mental health—she continued to have these outbursts. Her mother and father—partly from embarrassment in having such an odd daughter, and more because they would not or could not leaven her (blank)—withdrew more and more to themselves.

At the age of eleven she suddenly ceased her crying spells and her parents began to think her normal. When she began to dream at night, and in terror woke trembling to tell her dream— in detail—to their astonishment and horror her dream foretold disasters—invariably a few days later news headlines would blaze forth—and details would follow.

In horror they concealed her faculty.
....

A tall, slim young woman walked rapidly along a pleasant tree bordered road and turned in to a comfortable looking house. Her thin shoulders were rigid and her compressed lips and extreme pallor indicated that she was labouring under some strong emotion. She entered the house and glanced quickly into the downstairs rooms failing to find what she sought. She mounted the stairs and opened the door of a room in the front of the house.

"Mother," she burst out, "I simply can't go through with this—I love him too much—I won't burden him with it."

The woman raised her head from the mending on her lap and her face grew tired and older—

"But, Ruth dear, he loves you, and your father and I both think the change, the complete change would help you so much. We have done our best for you since you came to us—and all our love and care have not delivered you from your curse(?) (sic)."

"But Mother, it doesn't seem fair not to tell him...."

"Perhaps not, but he is a full grown man, a strong man, he is not as ordinary men—and once you are married he will care for you wisely and lovingly. He does care for you, you know—or I wouldn't consider the marriage."

The girl pulled nervously at her gloves—took them off and visibly the heat of her emotion faded and she (blank).

"I know," she said dully, "I know something will happen— I've been dreaming again for two nights—it isn't clear yet but it will come. It always does."

.....

The well dressed tired looking woman entered the doctor's office.

"Well, Jim, here I am again."

"Fran, you are my most (blank) patient."

"Yes, I know, I'm so difficult but I do feel so wretched. I'm sure there is something wrong."

"Nonsense, my dear, you need an interest in life—why don't you interest yourself in some worthy charities or adopt a child."

"I've tried the charities, and how can you ask me to take an unknown child with dear knows what ancestry and give him John's (blank)"

"My dear, these foibles went out of fashion long ago—if that is all...."

"All right then—I just can't do it. If that is all you can do for me I won't take up your time. Perhaps a change will help. I'll go down to the cottage for a while. The fall is beautiful down there.

"Good bye, Jim."

"Good bye, my dear, drop in to see me when you get back."

.....

Why do you torment me so. I do not love you.
The young lads hands clenched at the anguished tones.
The almost empty house re-echoed to the voices.

.....

I also found three old newspaper clippings in the summer of 1998 while sorting out my books. Brown with age, slightly damaged by being pinned together, and very different in content, the clippings were nestled between the pages of a well-thumbed and now ragged Bible. The handwritten inscription indicated the Bible was a 1922 Christmas gift to Dorothy Scott from her life long friend Grace Elliott.

The first of the pinned clippings was a poem, written by Abigail Cresson for the *New York Herald*, and was titled "Worry." A hole in the paper obliterated one word in the top line.

> *I spent (blank) hour*
> *In fear of the to-morrow;*
> *I grieved and wept,*
> *Anticipating sorrow.*

I knew no rest,
But when the morrow came;
Like other days
It seemed to be the same.

I laughed and mocked my fears—
They seemed so small,
I wondered that they broke
My rest at all.

Yet in my heart
A little doubt held sway—
What trouble might I meet
Another day?

Quite dark brown in colour, and seeming to be the oldest, the second item was entitled "How Many Can You Locate," and contained a list of Bible passages that "should be familiar to every Christian." The last clipping was from the *Lakeshore News'* "Social and Personals Column," and was a description of her daughter's bridal shower held at the home of one of her dear friends. Why did she keep these particular three clippings? What in their contents provided comfort or had a special meaning for her? I had hoped these treasured keepsakes would provide us with some insight, but I was unable to fathom the reasons for her choices.

Notwithstanding her emotional struggle, during the war years Mother was nevertheless able to accomplish a great deal. She became a wonderful cook and her children vividly recall her delicious meals and desserts. She stretched our food coupons imaginatively, canned fruits and vegetables, made jams and heavenly marmalade, and baked cookies by the dozens for the children. A competent seamstress and knitter, she made dresses for the girls and sweaters for the boys. With limited funds but lots of hard work, she redecorated the house, dyeing inexpensive cotton cloth for curtains and slipcovers and repainting rooms. She helped her husband with his sailboats and volunteered in various community projects, including collecting books for what eventually became the Pointe-Claire Public Library.

We Reminisce

As the war continued, Grandma and her employer moved to larger premises in a semi-detached house in Beaconsfield. Part of the Daoust farm, it had been constructed in 1780. She lived here for the longest time of any of her lodgings, in the comfort and familiarity of the farm location, near to her daughter and grandchildren. Warm friends and steady employment must have provided contentment and security after the unsettled Depression years.

In one of his letters, my brother remarked, "I remember visiting Grandma in Beaconsfield quite a few times on my bike. She was always welcoming, with my favourite cinnamon toast on offer—along with fresh milk, sometimes from the barn, in a bucket! The house there was kept spotlessly clean, but I never saw Grandma doing it.

"Mr. and Mrs. Daoust deserve honorable mention. I think because they were very good to her. They did not intrude on her privacy but always welcomed her when she approached them. Mrs. Daoust with her big smile of gold fillings would always come out from the back door when Grandma told her I was there. And Mr. Daoust would always make it possible to visit the animals."

I, too, remember the animals. A few cows and horses, enough to run the farm, but not too overwhelming in numbers for children unused to large animals. The garden was extensive, and Grandma had her own part of it for growing her beloved flowers and vegetables.

Mr. Daoust kept a big LaSalle car in half of the barn. I was allowed to accompany him for a polishing session, not to touch the car, but to admire. And admire I did. It was gorgeous. Big, and shiny, it smelled of leather and other expensive unknown materials. Mostly the car was used to taxi clerics, and we would stand by with awe when Mr. Daoust started up the powerful but quiet engine, and slowly turned the huge (to us) machine around on the driveway, getting ready to transport an important passenger.

The house was divided into two dwellings when Grandma lived there. I remember the thin walls allowing us to hear conversations filtering through from the other side. The house is now owned by the son of one of Grandma's dear friends, who has restored it to its original one-family residence. He lives there with his family. A few years ago he moved his business to his home, using as an office the area of the house that we remember as Grandma's kitchen and sunporch. He told me that he plans to keep the house renovations as consistent as possible with the original design.

What a happy thought that someone who cared for Grandma, even to the point of naming his daughter Kathleen Mary, is living in this lovely spot. Kathleen's name was affectionately given to another child, and friendly footsteps tread the same old floorboards.

At Mother's insistence one of the children began weekly visits to their Grandma at the farm. The conflict between the two women had long been felt by them and they had noticed Dorothy visited her mother as seldom as possible, making the children go in her place. We all remembered occasional feelings of resentment, as this duty was sometimes required when we would much rather have been playing with our friends. Dad accompanied his youngest daughter to Kathleen's house only once when she was about 12 years old. Something he said to the child during that half hour walk stayed in her mind, not so much the words themselves, but the way he had said it. Perhaps the family struggle had coloured his attitude that day.

I never saw Kathleen write a letter or receive one. It may have occurred, but I did not see it. Her reading matter was usually

Good Housekeeping and *Cosmopolitan* magazines. I remember a couple of books, but not their titles. She liked to knit, and created many beautiful items for her grandchildren, and later her great-grandchildren, while listening to the radio.

Busy physically, Kathleen spent long summer hours in her garden, sharing her harvest with family and friends. My favourites were Swiss chard, green beans and beefsteak tomatoes. Beautiful hollyhocks and pink flocks bordered the vegetables.

Climbing the south wall of Grandma's sun room were masses of blue morning glories tended by her magic fingers. Inside the glassed-in porch were abundant multi-coloured African violets, and in the summer the tables were crammed with cooling jars of goodies. Fruit was made into jams and preserves, which she poured into small jars and sealers. These were stored for the winter, when the taste of wild strawberry and raspberry jam was ambrosia in our plain diet.

Her house was immaculately clean, and her food delicious. Always using quality ingredients, she was a plain, but very good cook. She liked quality clothes, saved for their purchase, and carefully kept them for special events. Her favourite colour was blue.

My youngest brother claims that Grandma's radio favourites were Tennessee Ernie Ford and George Gobel. I hadn't remembered her choice but both entertainers were very popular at the time.

Kathleen and her neighbours became good friends. Many cups of strong tea were sipped in cozy kitchens. In warm weather, lemonade and cookies were shared in the shade of backyard gardens. She often spoke about the young neighbourhood children and their latest adventures or accomplishments. Her more elderly friends were kindly treated to small gifts from the garden, and hot baked or preserved goodies were delivered to them during bouts of illness or loneliness.

It was over one of our cups of tea that Grandma told me the story of cooking meals for Dr. Banting and Mr. Best when she was housekeeper for Jabez Elliott. I remember her saying that the young men looked as though they "needed feeding up." When we started looking into the plausibility of the story, we found that Dr. Banting was an associate of Dr. Elliott's at the University of Toronto. Both were researchers in internal medicine, and Dr. Banting was made a Fellow of the American College of Physicians at the same Philadelphia meeting when Dr. Elliott was named Vice-President. Two of the pall bearers at Dr. Elliott's funeral were contemporaries of Dr. Banting and were cited in Michael Bliss's book on Banting's life.

The History of Medicine Archives at University of Toronto sent me a letter which read in part:

Prof. Michael Bliss is a world's authority on Banting and Best... Prof. Bliss stated that although the story may very well be true there is no corroborating evidence that he is aware of, but both Dr. Banting and Mr. Best often dined around in those years and there seems no reason to doubt the story.

Through reading *The Discovery of Insulin,* I know that Prof. Bliss had had access to the Banting daily diaries. If he does not remember references to the names of families where Dr. Banting dined, the names were probably not included in the notes. The only source then would be the Elliott family guest book, which has not likely survived. Grandma's story, though, could very well be true.

Another story I heard just this summer was from a former neighbour and friend. She remembered Grandma saying she had once worked for someone who later, during World War II, became a dollar-a-year-man (prominent industrialists who helped with the war effort without salary). It took a little while, but she remembered his name—Beatty.

Edward Beatty, a lawyer from a wealthy family who attended the University of Toronto at the same time as Jabez Elliott, became President of CPR in 1924. After working his way up the ladder from the law department in 1901, he was instrumental in organizing the construction of CPR hotels across Canada. He formally opened the Royal York Hotel in Toronto on June 11, 1929, the day after Grandma began her work as a floor clerk in the hotel. Sir Edward had a suite of rooms where he stayed when he had meetings in Toronto and his suite was loaned out to special visitors in his absence.

Grandma would have included with her employment application a reference letter from Dr. Elliott attesting to her eight years of loyal service to his daughter and himself. His prominence in the city and Dr. Elliott's association with Mr. Beatty at the University of Toronto would have been viewed favourably. One of three scenarios were therefore possible in Grandma's story: first, that as President of CPR Mr. Beatty was, naturally, her employer, second, that Grandma worked on the floor where his suite was located, or third, his suite of rooms was in her area of responsibility. Grandma's story that she worked for Mr. Beatty holds up.

Comments by Mr. Beatty and Dr. Elliott's contemporaries such as "he still retained his deep and practical sympathy for those overtaken by life's mischances, and especially for the small and unimportant people," and, "the lives he has saved are legion, and the homes where his name was revered." This makes me believe that they were both essentially kind men—another reason why Grandma would have respected them. Remarkable, too, is that in the late 30's Grandma followed her daughter to the Lakeshore where, coincidentally, Mr. Beatty had a summer residence which he used until he died in March 1943. Dr. Elliott had died in 1942.

Some years before these deaths, close friends of our parents had become godparents to the first three children. One of my brothers recalls our godfather having a fierce disagreement with Dad because he had not joined the armed forces to serve overseas. Remembering how people felt about the war in 1939 and 1940 and remembering our godfather's strong personality, this recollection rings true. The other children remember snide comments from schoolmates whose fathers were serving in the armed forces.

Musing about the relationship between Mother's friends (our godparents) and Grandma, my brother said, "Grandma took over as a friend in place of Mother. Mother resented this greatly and told me once that Grandma always took over her girlfriends."

Mother's comment was not necessarily the full truth, and perhaps Kathleen's actions were not for the reasons Dorothy implies. We have another suggestion: the rift between the families could still have existed when our godfather came back from the war, suffering deeply after terrible experiences in the Canadian navy. We recall his ship was torpedoed at least three times, on the Murmansk run and in the Mediterranean. His health failed, and he took his own life. The reality of suicide was kept from the children by their parents, who substituted another reason for the death of their godfather. Schoolmates soon set my brother straight: "When I was hanging out with my friends the next day, they knew the truth."

We wonder if Mother, still angry about the disparagement of her husband, failed to comfort her friend at this crucial moment. Kathleen may have stepped into the breech doing what she could to help the bereaved family. Kathleen's timely intervention could have been perceived as interference by her daughter, a possible reason for her resentment, which increased as a strong bond developed between Grandma and our godmother. We also wonder if Kathleen had stepped into the breech more than once for her beloved young daughter, and this led to the comment about Grandma "always taking over" her girl friends.

We clearly remember Dad saying that he made great efforts trying to convince the editor of the local paper to protect the bereaved family and leave the story unpublished. The archives of the paper have not been checked to verify whether he was successful or not.

At every opportunity Dorothy disparaged her mother. Her bitterness caused great difficulty for the children, as they tried to remain loyal to both mother and grandmother. Kathleen never spoke an unkind word about her daughter, and was always available when needed.

My youngest brother remembers, "sometime in the 1940's when I attended elementary school, and we were living close to the village, Grandma would be home for me at lunch time. She made bread pudding for dessert, which I absolutely hated. I was about nine."

Where was Mother? Was she ill, and Grandma was helping the family once again?

One winter afternoon while one of her granddaughters was visiting, Grandma decided to wash her waist-length hair. Later, fascinated, the youngster watched her Grandma struggle with the long wet tangles for a few moments. Offering to help, she then parted and combed the straight grey strands, so different from her own curly hair, rearranging her grandmother's hair away from her face, over the tops of her ears and then slightly up from the nape of her neck. Pleased with the effect, before the end of the afternoon a new and very becoming style had been created. Grandma continued using this style the rest of her life.

When the war was over it was assumed that the children would work as soon as they were able, without neglecting their household chores. Dutifully Kathleen's oldest grandchild began working for a local dentist after classes and on weekends, contributing to the family finances. Since her high school was in Montreal West, travelling made for a very long day and was not easy for her, though I never once heard her complain. In the summer the teenager worked for the dentist full-time. Once her high schooling was completed, she entered a three-year nurses training program. With a strenuous 12-hour duty day and classes afterwards, it was a very hard program. With little or no money available from the family, and no emolument from the hospital, I have no idea how she managed. I doubt she even had bus fare to visit her parents or Grandma, even if she could spare the hours from her studies.

Other influences were now affecting the children, new demands were being made on their time, and there was a noticeable decrease in visits to their grandmother. It was a normal progression, yet difficult for Kathleen, as she had been so much a part of their lives up until now.

An additional financial burden affected the family in 1948, when as a result of some shenanigans by the owner of their rented home, they had to purchase a house. Government rules at the time permitted cancellation of a lease only in the event a family illness necessitated use by the owner. An illness was fabricated and shortly after we left, the house was sold. This improper use of the rules caused a great deal of anger in the family, but there was no way to amend the situation. We had to sell our beloved boat to raise the down payment. Grief stricken, we watched *Thalia Ann* leave the yacht club with a new owner.

Shortly after the family moved, another granddaughter finished her high school leaving exams and began working. Just like her father, she took the train downtown, then walked the remaining distance. But, once again, one of the children was contributing funds to the family. Money for train tickets for those still attending high school was, as always, a drain on the limited paycheck Dad was able to bring home. Salaries had not been markedly increased during the war and money for extras was simply not available.

Dad's continuing concern about finances led to serious discussions between our parents, resulting in a decision that Dad change his office management post for sales work. This meant taking a big risk, as he would be paid by commission, but the family had confidence he would be successful. And he was, beyond their wildest dreams. But it took time to establish himself, and in the beginning the budget was very tight. Grandma stayed with us in these lean times, and my brother remembered that she seemed to be suffering what was described as heart trouble.

He recollects that,"Grandma walked from our house to the doctor's on a hot summer day. Her heart rate was up as a result of her exertion (a normal occurrence) but the doctor diagnosed a heart conditon.

"Thereafter Grandma spent many hours on a chaise longue in the sun room at the front of the house. She did however, have terrible gas and belched continually. She was very worried about her non-existent heart condition. She was very testy and when I visited her once, home from school for lunch, she pronounced me as very nervous when I inadvertently rested a youthful and active foot on her chaise... As far back as I can remember, Grandma was plagued with digestive problems."

It is unknown if the cause was a legacy arising from her poor diet as a child in combination with her exposure to chemical toxicity in the munitions factory during the First World War.

And Then There Were Six

My sister completed her nursing degree, married a young man she had met through friends of our parents, and before the year was out Kathleen's first great-grandchild was born!

In contrast to the rest of the family Dorothy refused to visit or even speak to her daughter for two years. When one considers the very great lengths taken to hide the circumstances surrounding her own birth, perhaps Mother felt threatened by the baby's early arrival. The rejection was devasting to her daughter, and the wounds never completely healed. Grandma remained calm throughout, however, and showed utter delight at the child's existence. The next Christmas, Kathleen was pictured sitting in front of our fireplace holding this first great-grandson on her lap. Both subjects seemed intensely interested in each other. Unseen by the camera, the baby's mother was still enduring the silent treatment from our mother, Dorothy.

While this second conflict raged in the family, Grandma was being included less and less in the lives of her other grandchildren. They were finishing high school, working downtown or entering university. Grandma did not even attend any of the graduation exercises and we don't know why she was excluded from the ceremonies. Remembering her encouragement I think she would have been enormously pleased her grandchildren were able to complete high school and could look forward to greater opportunities than had been available for her.

Vestiges of the first mother-daughter conflict lingered for years. My brother told us that, when he was fifteen, Mom insisted he go to Beaconsfield for supper to celebrate Grandma's birthday. He was annoyed because it was race night at the Yacht Club, and he felt that Mom had a terrible love/hate relationship with grandma. When it was vital for Dorothy to visit Kathleen she still felt the need to protect herself from her mother's condemnation by using one of her children as buffer.

Very soon another granddaughter had accepted a proposal of marriage and received her engagement ring. On Easter weekend, 1952, the family moved back to the centre of the village. This comfortable newer house was constructed after the war, and was across the street from where Grandma had once lived with her employer.

Photographs of Grandma on the steps of the Beaconsfield farmhouse were probably taken in early summer of 1954.

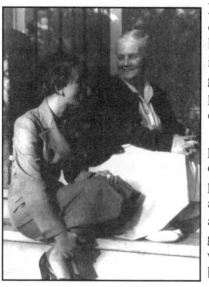

Kathleen is wearing a light dress and her favourite pale blue sweater. She is engrossed in conversation with her granddaughter, and they were probably talking about wedding plans.

Grandma carefully prepared for the wedding, the only time we can recall she participated in the wedding of a grandchild, or even attended a church service. She looked gorgeous standing with the wedding party, wearing a dark blue, almost navy coloured

110

dress, and a chic, broad brimmed picture hat and matching gloves. With her white hair, and pink and white complexion, she was stunning. The event was informal and relaxed, as the reception was held in the garden at home, and sitting at the head table Grandma appeared to enjoy every minute.

Kathleen's employer died in the mid-fifties and I was never sure whether she was glad or sorry. Quite matter-of-fact about her responsibilites and the services she was required to perform for the old gentleman, a professional always, she did not reveal very much about her feelings towards him. She would have had to consider new options for her financial survival though, and Dad would again provide counsel. A comfort, I am sure, was her love for a dark-haired tiny mite named Katie, a favourite neighbour from the moment Kathleen saw her as a newborn baby. We can't remember the exact date when she was born, but we remember Kathleen spent hours with the baby as she learned to walk and talk. Another "Katie!"

Changes were coming fast now in Kathleen's family. Her second great-grandchild was born in early January 1953, her grandsons were working far from home during the summers and one granddaughter and her new husband had moved to Toronto. Visiting one Christmas they stayed with Grandma, who was living alone after the death of her employer, and they slept in the vacant downstairs bedroom. Her third great-grand-child was born in April of 1955, and Grandma fortunately was free to take care of the other children while their mother was in the hospital. Four female generations were later captured in a beautiful photograph, with the three mothers gazing fondly

at the tiny child. And the next fall Katie's fourth great-grand-child was born in Toronto.

The Toronto contingent came to the Lakeshore for Christmas with their three-month-old son. It was his first introduction to his great-grandmother although he had met his grandparents when they visited Toronto earlier in the year. His aunt, uncomfortably pregnant again and wearing a bright red maternity top, was described by her brother as "a tired red robin!" Kathleen's fourth great-grandson was born the spring of 1956 in Montreal and another great-granddaughter was born the following November in Toronto. She now had six great-grandchildren.

Six great-grandchildren! She must have been thrilled. The lonely rejected orphan, who had faced unbelieveable difficulties since the age of six, and had survived by her own courage and determination, now had a family of 16 and numerous close friends.

Grandma managed to spend time with all her great-grandchildren over the years, and all of them remember her fondly. Her knitting needles were always flying, as she created wonderful winter accessories to be presented at Christmas time. One of the children vividly remembers the beautiful blue scarf and toque her great-grandmother made for her. A favourite ensemble, it was ever so carefully tended for use each year. Another remembers that "Grandma made me a gorgeous jerkin, knitting strands of different coloured wools together. It was a lovely, warm garment, and I wore it for years."

She remained at the farm after the death of her employer, and the son of a close friend lodged with her for two summers while he worked locally. He later named his first daughter Mary Kathleen after our Grandma. He vividly remembers the delicious potato and onion soup she used to make as well as a rich rice pudding made with fresh farm eggs and cream.

My youngest brother remembers, "He was a couple of years older than me and I liked him, but I had feelings of envy for Grandma's closeness to him."

"A young English couple were lodged in the upstairs rooms for a time," he recalls. "Grandma thought they were filthy for bathing together in the downstairs bathroom. She hated British people anyway."

As her grandchildren reached adulthood, it must have been a difficult adjustment for Kathleen. Her grandsons had been very absorbed with getting their education and starting their business careers, and then were transferred out of province. One granddaughter had moved to Toronto, and was engrossed in bringing up her two children. The other granddaughter was living locally, but had the responsibilites of four young children as well as the demands of husband and home.

During these years, Kathleen would see her grandchildren less and less and certainly not on the daily or weekly basis to which she had become accustomed. She missed their presence, as the children and their welfare had been her focus for so many years.

As well, Dad's business became increasingly prosperous, and he and Mother began a succession of annual convention trips, and long vacations to Florida. The Florida trips eventually culminated in the purchase of a home in Daytona Beach.

Kathleen, her strength diminishing, became less and less involved in family activities as she grew older. She lived a modest, quiet life in Beaconsfield, with occasional visits by family members, and annual gatherings for Christmas, anniversaries and birthdays. Always looking neat and tidy, wearing her favourite colour, blue, crowned by her beautiful white hair, she presided as matriarch of the now large group of relatives. Everyone had an opportunity for a quiet word with her, and she seemed rather bemused as she surveyed what she had wrought.

There was a darker side to Kathleen, though, that would emerge when she felt herself slighted by family or friends. As mentioned earlier, she could express her displeasure very harshly. Just such an occasion occurred when Grandma chastised my sister for infrequent visits. The verbal attack has never been forgotten, nor the difficulties of organizing four young children and transportation to make these visits possible. Probably resenting

her perceived neglect by the family after her years of commitment to them, it is not surprising that Kathleen expressed her
dismay in this manner. It was particularly unfortunate, though,
that this granddaughter was the recipient of her outburst. The
changes in family situations were not, after all, her doing. But
she happened to be with Kathleen, and took the brunt of the
anger on behalf of the whole family.

Grandma began mentioning vague symptoms of discomfort.
One letter addressed to her in August of 1959 confirms that she
was at least able to continue living on the farm. I suspect Dad
was helping to make this possible. His loyalty and tenderness to
his mother-in-law never wavered.

Celebrating Christmas in 1960, a photograph shows Grandma
sitting in her favourite chair in front of the fireplace. Oscar, the
family cat, is sleeping comfortably on Grandma's broad lap.
Everyone had been able to get home safely for the holidays that
year, including our London-based brother, though it had been an
incredibly wild, stormy time for travelling. The intensity of our
celebrations and delight at being together for those few days was
not easily forgotten. We repeated its joy nearly 40 years later
when Cedar Park School held a centennial anniversary weekend.
The passage of time made no difference in our delight, even if
our energy had diminished somewhat. We felt so lucky.

Grandma's health soon began to deteriorate, and we worried
about all the stairs she had to climb at the farm. She tried living
with her daughter. It didn't work out and she was eventually
installed in a small, more convenient local apartment. She had to
give up her beloved dog and companion, Duffy, before moving
though, which must have caused her considerable grief. Close
friends came to the rescue and kindly offered Duffy a home.

The Toronto contingent of four was transferred back to
Montreal in 1962 and rented a split level on the North Shore.
One of the children remembers, "sitting on newspapers in our
sparsely furnished living room stripping dry summer savory
leaves from plants which Grandma had grown and later dried."

While we lived in Pierrefonds and our parents were on one of their extended trips we visited Kathleen at her apartment, finding her unwell. Concerned at her condition, we packed her up and took her home to stay with us. After a few days she seemed to revive, began involving herself in family activities, eating dinner with us, taking walks in the garden, and showing interest in the children.

When Dorothy returned from her trip, she immediately removed Kathleen and took her back to her apartment. Our offer to have Kathleen stay longer was curtly refused. Curious, as Kathleen was enjoying herself. And then there was 1964, a very eventful year for the family....

The family's Lakeshore home was sold in March, one son was transferred farther afield to Vancouver and the other son married his beloved in Kemi, Finland. They had met on the Channel ferry returning to England after holidaying on the Continent. Once the Finnish church was satisfied the young man was acceptable as a partner for one of their parishioners, the marriage was celebrated in the bride's home town with her family and friends. Only one of our family was able to make the trip to

Finland for the wedding, and he gallantly stood by his brother on the momentous day. The couple honeymooned in Lapland, above the Arctic Circle.

Later in the spring, construction was started on a family vacation house near Sutton and when it was completed in the fall Dad and Mum moved to their new country home, while still maintaining a Lakeshore apartment.

I remember a particularly harrowing time as a result of the sale of the Lakeshore house. Mother had a nervous breakdown and took to her bed when she heard the sale was final. The house had been on the market for only a few days, and she was to be uprooted in a matter of weeks. Dad's usual solution when faced with these situations was to take Mother on a trip. This time he couldn't as the move had priority.

When I visited her for the first time after the sale, she was in bed, sobbing. I held her hand and tried to soothe her, asking what was the matter. It was hard for me to understand what was going on. She was so sorry the house had been sold, but surely, I thought, this had been discussed and decided between my parents. Why, then, was she so devastated? Nevertheless, when I spoke words of comfort, she said, "You understand." But what did I understand? She had loved the house, and mourned its loss.

It was much later, in fact, when we were delving into her early history, that we began to pick up clues that suggested the loss of her favourite home meant a great deal more. It was a real bereavement, and perhaps she was connecting to events in her early childhood that made her very unhappy. Her distress was, perhaps, anticipation of a recurrence of her sense of abandonment. Even though Dad was still with her, and they were only changing houses, maybe she was still emotionally vulnerable.

We suspect Grandma may have left her daughter with Aunt Sarah in Ottawa while she sought employment in Toronto. Dorothy knew nothing of her father and her attachment to her mother would have been very strong. The loss of her mother when she was so young would have been devastating. Aunt Sarah Adams was elderly and it may have been extremely difficult for Dorothy to adjust to the new situation. While Kathleen may have understood some of her child's feelings, earning a living was an urgent necessity. Lack of opportunity in Ottawa may have made the search for employment in the larger city imperative. And considering her own experiences as an orphan, she may have felt Dorothy was in a fortunate and comfortable situation with Aunt Sarah.

My sister felt that, "Dorothy's feelings of powerlessness in the face of Dad's decision to sell the house without consultation may have also led to her extreme reaction. He said they were only going to find out how much the house was worth. It was sold at once and Dad wanted to move to Sutton full-time, but I doubt that she did. It would be a lonely existence for her."

"Dad did not consider Mother at all on this, did he!" exclaims another brother. "The house had meant a lot to Mom because living there was a happier period in her life. She no longer had to contend with Grandmother Bessie, who stayed with us regularly, nor Grandma Scott who had stayed with us for a period when she had her ill-diagnosed heart problem. Mom loved the rose garden out front and the lilac trees."

I sensed while writing this story that Grandma had always kept a watchful eye over her beloved daughter. A pattern of constant visits, regular picture taking, and Dad's courtliness towards his mother-in-law, also support this view. When grandchildren appeared on the scene, she was always there to help. When they were older and visited Kathleen at her home, the first question always was "How's your mother?" Gifts of flowers, vegetables, jams, jellies and magazines, were always being sent home for her.

There is no doubt the conflict between the two women ebbed and flowed. Perhaps they never really understood each other, nor understood how their childhood experiences might have affected their attitudes.

The next big event in 1964 was Katie's grandson coming home from England bringing his new wife. A fabulous picture taken at Sutton that Christmas captures the moment—Grandma, com-

pletely enveloped by members of her own family, glowing with happiness. It is a beautiful portrait of a proud matriarch. And she didn't know it at the time, but four more children would eventually be added to the immediate family complement giving her a total of ten great-grandchildren. Neither the tiny orphan leaving Scotland nor the struggling single mother in Toronto could ever have envisioned this in her future.

Celebrating Christmas at my house in 1966, Grandma was photographed with an attentive son-in-law beside her at the festive dinner table. My youngest brother, home from the west on a short vacation, was also present, an additional pleasure for all of us. On his way back to Vancouver, my brother noticed a beautiful young lady in the airport waiting for the same flight. After inquiring, he was given her seat number by the ticket agent. Naturally he selected a seat across the aisle. Voila! He became acquainted with his future wife!

Epilogue

*A*bout 1967, at age 81 and with failing health, Grandma was no longer able to live in an apartment by herself. Mum experimented with foster family accommodation for her in the Eastern Townships. One of these homes where Grandma lived was infused with the pungent odour of dog food being cooked in one of the kitchens, because the landlady was raising West Highland terriers. The smell permeating the house was very unpleasant to my sensitive nose and I wondered how Grandma coped. She had no complaint however and told me the landlady was very kind to her.

Others, however, remember Grandma as a very difficult boarder. Dislocated again in her life, resenting her infirmities and diminishing contact with her family, those in direct contact were made clearly aware of her unhappiness. The small, ten-year-old child who was tactfully described by Quarriers as "self-willed," retained this habit, now exacerbated in the older, unhappy woman. It made those around her extremely uncomfortable.

Dad and Mum gave up their Lakeshore apartment to live in Sutton year round, which was much closer to Kathleen's foster homes. In their Sutton guest book dated July 23, 1968 we read "Grandma at Sutton for her birthday." Three months later, my youngest brother was married in the Town of Mount Royal. Unfortunately, Grandma was not well enough to attend the ceremony. When Grandma was feeling better, the young couple, visiting from their home in Calgary, took her on a tour of Granby Zoo. They commented, "Grandma had a very good time. She really enjoyed all the cats!"

With one grandson in Calgary, one in Toronto, one granddaughter in a full body cast with a back injury, and the other struggling with family problems, Grandma would not be seeing her grandchildren frequently. However, in March of 1969 my sister wrote in the guest book, "Visited Grandma this a.m. She looks well and happy."

Two weeks later Kathleen's eighth great-grandchild was born in Toronto. Grandma lived long enough to appreciate these first eight children, but numbers nine and ten were born several years after her death. However, Katie would have been very pleased to know that her family line continues to grow, and that there are now six great-great-grandchildren growing up in Ontario, Quebec and the United States.

In another guest book entry dated July 23, 1969, a dear friend of Grandma remarks, "Beautiful day—Kathleen's 80th birthday. Lovely visit. G. M."

None of us knew then that July 23, 1969 was really her 83rd birthday. I don't think even she knew her correct birth date. After all, no documents were ever issued to the orphans who came to Canada, and a frightened six-year-old entering an orphanage in 1892 couldn't be expected to remember these details.

My sister and I were working full time by August 1969, one brother was living in Calgary, and Katie's eldest grandson, visited his parents in August of 1969 with his wife and two children, then boarded a plane for England. They had been transferred again, and would not return to live in Canada.

I wonder how she felt about her grandchildren's new lives which made visits with her so difficult to arrange. With her health and memory failing, perhaps she was accepting with equanimity the visits they were able to make.

Sometime in her 84th year, Grandma was placed in a nursing home near a town called Melbourne near Richmond, which was quite a bit further east but still in the province of Quebec. Why Melbourne? It seemed so far away and much less accessible for family visits. For years we have wondered about Dorothy's placement choice for her mother and speculated on the reasons for it. Was this nursing home her only option at the time? Had their conflict of years standing played a role in her decision? Was this Katie's ultimate betrayal by family?

Alone and isolated at Melbourne far from grandchildren now scattered on two continents, visited occasionally by her daughter and infrequently by the grandchildren, Kathleen must have wondered about the harsh hand life had dealt her. Removed from her family at age six, eighty years later the circle had closed, and once again she was on her own, away from the bosom of her family, living with strangers.

And yet, when my sister and her family visited in May of 1971, Grandma seemed well and reasonably content. She walked the grounds with them, showing them the farm animals and her favourite kitten, chatting amicably about points of interest on the property. We also visited Grandma at Melbourne that summer. Unaware that her life was soon to end, we were pleased she seemed well and comfortable, and looked forward to our next trip to that part of the country to see her.

The last picture of Grandma was taken on the front lawn of La Residence de Melbourne, sitting under a tree with her granddaughter and two teenaged great-grandchildren. Wearing a light summer dress and her favourite pale blue sweater, Grandma's

hair is very white, but the resolute expression on her aged face is very similar to the one captured on the ten-year-old's 1896 arrival in Canada. She appears fearful, yet determined to be brave.

My sister visited again in October. Grandma was confined to bed and her mind was wandering. My sister's impression that day was that Grandma appeared to have no regret, no fear, and was ready for the struggle to end. My sister said later, "She had given up, I think. In a moment of lucidity she said to me, 'I'm dying, you know. 83 years old—not bad for this old sinner.'"

After nearly eighty-six years of life, Catherine Walls Scott, whom her grandchildren knew as their Grandma Kathleen Wales Scott, died on December 9, 1971. Two days later with her Canadian family honouring her, Katie was buried in Grace Church Cemetery at Sutton, Quebec.

We make our lives whether of peace or confusion, out of given material. What will be given, we can neither know nor arrange.
—Howard Spring

Sources

Books and Articles

Archives of Ontario. *Librarians Guide to Microfilm Information.* Interloan Service, Toronto: June 28, 1994.

Bagnall, Kenneth. *The Little Immigrants.* Toronto: Macmillan of Canada, 1980.

Birkett, Patricia. *Checklist of Parish Registers.* 4th Edition. Ottawa: National Archives of Canada Manuscript Division, 1987.

Bliss, Michael. *The Discovery of Insulin.* Toronto: McClelland and Stewart, 1982.

Brack, Arthur. "Basic Family Research." Based on the recording of the talk given to the Anglo-Scottish Family History Society. Manchester Genealogist, October, 1992.

Brockville Recorder and Times. "A Fairknowe Home Girl shot." July 15, 1896.

Broughton, Dawn. "LDS Branch Genealogical Libraries in Ontario." *Families.* 25.4 (1986): 199-205.

Burges, Alex. "Arrival of Children in Canada." *The Mail,* Glasgow, Scotland, April 13, 1895. National Archives of Canada: film C-4709.

Burnett, Frances Hodgson. *The Head of the House of Coombe.* Toronto: McClelland and Stewart, 1922.

Burnett, Frances Hodgson. *Robin.* Toronto: McClelland and Stewart, 1922.

Canadian Pacific Railway. *Canadian Pacific Facts and Figures.* compiled and edited by the Department of Public Relations. Montreal: Canadian Pacific Foundation Library, 1946. pp.40-42.

Cox, Ron. *1871 Ontario Census/Electoral Districts, Townships, Wards, Counties and Associated Microfilm.* Pointe-Claire: Quebec Family History Society, 1996.

"Archibald Alison 1757-1839"; "Sir Archibald Alison 1792-1867"; "William Pulteney Alison 1790-1859." *Dictionary of National Biography.* England, pp. 286-290.

Edwards, Trent. "Ceremony Honours British Home Children." *Ottawa Citizen.* June 15, 1998.

Elliott, Bruce S.. *Tracing Your Ottawa Family.* Ottawa: Corporation of the City of Ottawa, 1984.

Fitzgerald, Doris M.. *Thornhill 1793-1963, The History of an Ontario Village.* Thornhill, 1964.

Trotsky, Susan M., ed. *Contemporary Authors.* Vol. 136 Detroit: Gale Research Inc., 1992. pp. 65.

Gladstone-Millar, Lynne. *The Colinton Story: 900 Years of a Scottish Parish*. Edinburgh: Saint Andrew Press, 1994.

Harrison, Phyllis. *The Home Children*. Winnipeg: Watson & Dwyer Publishing Ltd., 1979.

Harvey, Sir Paul, ed. "Sir Archibald Alison 1792-1867." *Oxford Companion to English Literature*. 4th Edition. New York: Oxford University Press, 1969. pp. 18.

Horn, Pamela. "The Emigration of Pauper Children to Canada 1870-1914." *Genealogists Magazine*. 25.10 (1997): 393-399.

House of Commons. "Select Committee Report, Health - Third Report." Westminster: House of Commons, July 1998.

Humphreys, Margaret. *Empty Cradles*. Corgi Edition. London: Transworld Publishers, 1995.

Lamb, W. Kaye, *History of the Canadian Pacific*. New York: MacMillan Publishing Company Incorporated, 1977.

Lorente, David and Kay. "An Update on the Home Children." *Anglo-Celtic Annals, British Isles Family History Society of Greater Ottawa Conference Proceedings*. Ottawa, 1996. pp. 22-25.

Lorente, David. *Home Children Research Kit*. Renfrew: Home Children Canada Committee, Heritage Renfrew, 1997.

Lorente, David and Kay. "Home Children Canada." Updates published at intervals by Heritage Renfrew Opeongo Lines, Renfrew, 1997-1999.

Lovell, John and Son. "Wales, Ontario." "Blackstock, Ontario." *The Gazetteer of the Dominion of Canada*, Montreal: Lovell's, 1908. pp. 936, 316.

Matthews, Brian R.. *A History of Pointe-Claire*. Pointe-Claire: Brianor Ltd., 1985.

McGill, Jean S.. *A Pioneer History of the County of Lanark*. Toronto: T.H. Best Printing Co. Ltd., 1968.

Merriman, Brenda Dougall. *Genealogy in Ontario: Searching the Records*. 3rd Edition. Toronto: The Ontario Genealogical Society, 1996.

Miller-Barstow, D.H.. *Beatty of the CPR*. Toronto: McClelland and Stewart Limited, 1951.

Mitchell, John Fowler and Sheila. *West Fife Monumental Inscriptions pre-1855*. Edinburgh: Scottish Genealogy Society, 1971.

Morrison, Leonard A. *The History of the Alison or Allison Family in Europe and America A.D. 1135-1893*. Boston: Damrell & Upham, 1893.

Morton, Desmond and J.L. Granatstein. *Marching to Armageddon, 1914-1918*. Toronto: Lester & Orpen Denys, 1989.

O'Neill, Juliet. "Home Children to Receive Apology." *Ottawa Citizen*, August 1, 1998.

O'Neill, Juliet. "Giving Home Children a Past." *Ottawa Citizen*, August 9, 1998.

Ontario Genealogical Society. *Albert Street Cemetery, Arnprior.* Ottawa: OGS, 1978.

Ontario Genealogical Society. *Auld Kirk Cemetery, Almonte,* Ottawa: OGS, 1980.

Ontario Genealogical Society. *Beechwood Cemetery 1901-1930.* Ottawa: OGS, 1993.

Ontario Genealogical Society. *Beechwood Cemetery 1931-1955.* Ottawa: OGS, 1995.

Ontario Genealogical Society. *Kitley Census 1851.* Brockville: Stormont, Dundas & Glengarry Branch OGS, 1990.

Ontario Genealogical Society. *Kitley Census 1861,* Brockville: Stormont, Dundas & Glengarry Branch OGS, 1992.

Parr, Joy. *Labouring Children: British Immigrant Apprentices to Canada.* London: Croom Helm, 1980.

Quarrier, William. "New Years Letter to our Children and Friends in Canada." *Orphans Home of Scotland.* Bridge of Weir. Renfrew, 1897. pp. 1-4. National Archives Immigration Film C-4709.

Quarrier, William. "Our Second Band of Children to Canada This Year." *Orphans Home of Scotland.* May 29, 1896.

Quarrier, William. "Untitled." *Quarrier Archives.* Bridge of Weir, Renfrew, Scotland. June 3,9,15, 1896. pp.40-41.

Quarrier, William. "Girls for the Home." *Brockville Recorder and Times,* June 5, 1896.

Read, Donald E.. "Canadian Post Office Records for the Genealogist." *Families*. 25.3 (1986): 133.

Renardson, Wayne C.. "The National Resources Mobilization Act, 1940." *Families*. 28 (1989): 37-40.

Roy, Janine. *Tracing Your Ancestors in Canada*. Ottawa: National Archives of Canada, 1993.

Thompson, F.L.M.. *The Rise of Respectable Society—A Social History of Victorian Britain 1830-1900*. Cambridge: Harvard University Press, 1988.

Trudel, Monique. "Union List of Canadian Newspapers." National Library of Canada Newspaper Section, Ottawa, 1977.

The United Church of Canada Committee on Archives and History. *Guide to Family History Research in the Archival Repositories of the United Church of Canada*. Toronto: Ontario Genealogical Society, 1996.

Wagner, Gillian. *Children of the Empire*. London: Weidenfeld & Nicolson,1982.

"Sir Archibald Alison 1826-1907." *Who Was Who*. Vol. 1 (1897-1915). London: A. & C. Black, 1920.

Wilson, Rev. John. *Gazetteer of Scotland*. Milton: Global Heritage Press, 1999.

Official Records and Other Sources

"And We Knew How to Dance." National Film Board of Canada, 1993.

Anglican Diocese Office, Toronto. "Baptismal Records." computer search, 1909-1915.

Anglican Diocese Office, Ottawa. "Baptismal Records." computer search, 1909-1915.

Auld Kirk Presbyterian Church, Ramsay Township, Lanark County. "Congregation Records: births, marriages, deaths, communicants, membership lists, 1833-1926." *National Archives of Canada Parish Records*. Film M-2217.

Bank Street Presbyterian Church, Ottawa. "Baptismal Record: Florence Bell Adams." July 11, 1900.

Beechwood Cemetery Archives, Ottawa. "Burial record extracts: Florence Bell Adams," September 19, 1902.

Beechwood Cemetery Archives, Ottawa. "Burial record extracts: William H. Adams." November 26, 1909

Beechwood Cemetery Archives, Ottawa. "Burial record extracts: William Scott." June 19, 1915.

Fairknowe Receiving and Distributing Home, Brockville. Orphan Homes of Scotland, William Quarrier. "Lists and Reports 1893-1942." National Archives of Canada Immigration films RG 76, C-4709, C-4710. File 1532.

"For You Alone." Composer Henry E. Geehli. Lyrics by P.J. O'Reilly. McGill Faculty of Music Archives, Montreal.

"Immigration of Children Inspection Lists and Reports, 1874-1903." *National Archives of Canada.* films C-4733, 1874-1896; C-4797, 1896-1901; C-7320, 1896-1900; C-7345, 1898-1900; C-7380, 1900-1902; C-7814, 1902; C-7815, 1898-1903.

Land Registry Office, Ottawa-Carleton County. "Abstract Indexes: Slater St. Lot 43, P3922, 1866-1984. Gordon St. Lot 5, P33446, 1890-1995." County Court House, Elgin St., Ottawa.

Land Registry Office, Ottawa-Carleton County. "Lots 3922, 33446. Extracts: Deeds, Bargain and Sales, Mortgages and Wills. Adams and Huband families." County Court House, Elgin St., Ottawa.

"Obituary: Mrs. Mabel Tait Elliot." *Toronto Daily Star.* July 28, 1922.

"Obituaries: William H. Adams, Nov. 25, 1909; Sarah Adams, Dec. 27, 1930; Mrs. Annie Hamilton, Jan. 8, 1914; Mrs. R. Hornidge, July 13, 1933." *The Ottawa Journal.*

Ontario. "Birth, marriage and death record extracts for the Adams, Hamilton, Hornidge, Kinnaird, MacDougall and Scott families." Ontario Archives, Grenville St., Toronto.

Ontario. Birth registration June 15, 1909(1967). Marriage registration June 30, 1928. Dorothy Scott. Registrar General's Office, Thunder Bay.

Ontario. "Canadian Expeditionary Force, First World War." Personnel file. Hector MacDougall. Personnel Records Unit, National Archives of Canada, Ottawa.

Ontario. "Census films 1851-1901." National Archives of Canada, Ottawa.

Ontario. "City Directories 1896-1930." City of Ottawa Archives.

Ontario. "Federal Electoral Enumeration List 1935." Danforth Riding, Urban Affairs Library, Metro Hall, Toronto.

Ontario. "Parish records 1846-1852, 1863-1913: births, marriages, deaths, members." St. Andrews Presbyterian Church of Scotland, Kitley Township, Leeds County. Film H-1810. National Archives of Canada, Ottawa.

Ontario. "Post Office Employment records. Stormont Electoral District—Woodlands. RG3, D3. Employment record Robert H. Stuart 1864-1909." National Archives Client Services and Communications Branch, National Archives, Ottawa.

Ontario. "Stormont County Presbyterian Parish Records, Osnabruck and Lunenburg Congregations 1848-1909." Film C-3030. National Archives of Canada, Ottawa.

Ontario. "Surrogate Court Estate File, Carleton County 1931. Sarah Adams RG22 14911-3 1931, 3816 A6141/B-10/S-3/C-10." Ontario Archives, Toronto.

Ontario. *Vital Statistics.* "Births, marriages, deaths 1869-1924." Filmed Index. Ontario Archives, Toronto.

Quarrier Home Children. S.S. Siberian group photographed on arrival at Fairknowe, Brockville, June 1896. Kindness of Mrs. Grace Bruce, Ottawa.

"Quarrier Homes 1892 Admission record. Catherine Walls Scott." Quarrier Archives, Bridge of Weir, Renfrewshire.

Scotland. "Birth, marriage and death extracts: Old Parish Registers. East Lothian, Fife and Midlothian. Scott, Smith and Walls families." General Register Office, Edinburgh.

Scotland. "Birth and marriage extracts: Old Parish Registers. Fossoway and Tulliebolle. Walls family." Church of Jesus Christ of Latter Day Saints, Family History Department, Salt Lake City.

Scotland. "Birth & marriage certificate facsimiles: Scott and Smith families." General Register Office, Edinburgh.

Scotland. "Births and marriages to 1874." Fiche index: East Lothian, Fife, Lanark, Midlothian, Perth, Fossoway, Tulliebolle. International Genealogical Index. Church of Jesus Christ of Latter Day Saints, Salt Lake City.

Scotland. "Census 1851-1891: Scott, Smith and Walls families." General Register Office, Edinburgh.

Scotland. "County Directories 1882-1896: Woodville." General Register Office, Edinburgh.

Scotland. "Kirk Session Records." Colinton Parish Church, Colinton, Midlothian.

Scotland. *Ordinance Survey Map*. Scotland 6" County series. Ordinance Map Office, Southampton, England, 1852. Revised 1877. National Library of Scotland, Edinburgh.

Scotland. "Sheet 6—Edinburghshire 1850." *Victorian Ordinance Survey Map.* Updated 1895. Caledonian Books, Collieston, Ellon, Aberdeenshire, 1998.

"Ship Passenger List Arrivals." S.S. Siberian, June 8, 1896. Film: C-4541. National Archives of Canada, Ottawa.

"Ship Passenger List Departures 1890-1960." BT27-205. S.S. Siberian May 29, 1896. Public Records Office, Kew, England.

Toronto Board of Education. "School admission records 1921-1923." Records Management Services, Harbord & Huron St.

"Toronto City Directories 1902-1941." Might Directories. Film: Ontario Archives, Grenville St., Toronto. Toronto Public Library, Yonge St., Toronto.

Trinity Methodist Church. "Baptismal, membership & Sunday School records, 1909-1912." Trinity-St. Paul's United Church, Bloor St., Toronto.

United Church of Canada. "Burial extract 1971. Sutton-Dunham Pastoral Charge." Sutton, Quebec.

United Church of Canada. "Ottawa baptisms 1909-1915." Montreal & Ottawa Conference Archives, Ottawa.

United Church of Canada. "Toronto baptisms 1909-1912." United Church Archives, Toronto.

University of Toronto. Newspaper clippings. "Jabez Henry Elliott, M.B. 1897." File A73-0026/098(062), University Archives, Toronto.

University of Toronto. "Letter July 12, 1999." History of
Medicine Program. Department of History/History of
Medicine, Toronto.

Acknowledgements

This book could not have been completed without the encouragement of my sister and my two brothers, and I am enormously grateful to them.

A special note of thanks must also go to Daniel Parkinson of Toronto, Alan J.L. MacLeod of Edinburgh, Hugh Banfill of Pointe-Claire, and the staff of Ottawa City Archives, the Ottawa Branch of the Ontario Genealogical Society, the Pointe-Claire Library and the Quebec Family History Society.

AGMV Marquis

MEMBER OF THE SCABRINI GROUP

Quebec, Canada
2001